# *Spies* *in* REVOLUTIONARY RHODE ISLAND

# *Spies* *in* REVOLUTIONARY RHODE ISLAND

CHRISTIAN M. McBURNEY

THE History PRESS

Published by The History Press
Charleston, SC 29403
www.historypress.net



*Front cover, top left*: Major General John Sullivan. *Author's Collection. Front cover, top middle*: The landing of the French troops in Newport on July 11, 1780. *Library of Congress. Front cover, top right*: General Sir Henry Clinton. London, 1780. *Anne S.K. Brown Military Collection, John Hay Library. Front cover, bottom*: The British frigate *Rose* took on board escaped Loyalists, as well as spies. *Image of operational copy of the ship from John Fitzhugh Millar.*
*Back cover, top*: *A Topographical Chart of the Bay of Narragansett* by Charles Blaskowitz, London, 1777. *Library of Congress. Back cover, inset*: *The Capture of General Prescott. Catherine Williams,* Biography of Revolutionary Heroes *(1839). Back cover, bottom*: *The Siege of Rhode Island, taken from Mr. Brindley's House on the 25th of August, 1778.* From *Gentleman's Magazine*, London, February 1779. *Author's collection.*

First published 2014

Manufactured in the United States

ISBN 978.1.62619.724.4

Library of Congress Cataloging-in-Publication Data

McBurney, Christian M.
Spies in revolutionary Rhode Island / Christian M. McBurney.
pages cm
Includes bibliographical references and index.
ISBN 978-1-62619-724-4 (paperback)
1. Rhode Island--History--Revolution, 1775-1783--Secret service. 2. United States--History--Revolution, 1775-1783--Secret service. 3. Spies--Rhode Island--History--18th century. 4. Spies--Rhode Island--Biography. 5. Espionage, British--Rhode Island--History--18th century. 6. Spies--Great Britain--Biography. I. Title.
E279.M35 2014
973.3'85--dc23
2014036071

# Contents

# Preface

Outside of New York City, and possibly Philadelphia, no theater of war during the American Revolution produced such rich stories of spies and spying as Rhode Island. During two stretches, the state was a particular hotbed of espionage: from December 1776 to October 1779, when the British army occupied Newport (along with the rest of Aquidneck Island and Conanicut Island), and from July 1780 to August 1781, when French forces occupied the port city. At the time, Newport was one of the five most important commercial ports of the former thirteen colonies and boasted North America's best harbor for a fleet of large warships.

Rhode Island spies proved both notorious and daring. One was caught and hanged in Providence by American authorities. Another, whose betrayals nearly reached the level of Benedict Arnold's, toiled in the heart of Providence and met Continental army officers without ever being discovered. One Patriot spy worked in the midst of British-occupied Aquidneck Island for more than a year without being caught. Several other spies, fleeing from French-occupied Newport, made daring escapes on small boats before providing the top British commanders with valuable intelligence. Three prominent spies were women—one of whom plied her trade disguised as a peddler.

The stakes were high. During the British occupation of Newport, if the Americans could have invaded and captured the Newport garrison, the victory could have ended the war. Later, when the French occupied Newport in July 1780, the stakes increased. Henry Clinton, the British commander

*The Unfortunate Death of Major André.* Hanging was typically the fate of spies caught in disguise, including British major John André, hanged in 1780 by the Americans. *Anne S.K. Brown Military Collection, John Hay Library.*

in chief of all North American forces, personally received reports from spies embedded in Newport on the movements of the French fleet and their defenses in Rhode Island in preparation for his own planned invasion of Newport. A British victory, he thought, could drive the hated but powerful French out of the war.

The stakes were high for the spies on a personal level too. They risked being caught and sentenced to die by hanging, the traditional punishment for convicted spies. Accordingly, that made the ongoing role of spy a dangerous occupation.

The problem both of the opposing sides faced in attempting to identify spies in their midst was that the American Revolution was not only a rebellion against Crown rule, it was also a civil war. On one side were the supporters of King George III—called Loyalists by the British and Tories by the Patriots. On the other side were the supporters of independence from British rule—called "Whigs" by Patriots and "rebels" by the British. Whigs and Loyalists were drawn from the same people—it was almost impossible to distinguish between them. Each side had family members whose Rhode Island descendants went back to the mid-1600s. That was the case for Loyalist spy Thomas Hazard, for example; and his wife, Eunice, was a great-granddaughter of founder Roger Williams.

This book contains the first detailed description of the extraordinary espionage activities surrounding Clinton's bold plan to attack the French fleet and army that landed at Newport on July 11, 1780, as well as the subsequent feints and actions taken by the opposing forces while the French occupied Newport. While small parts of the story have appeared in various history books on spies, the entire story of these clandestine operations has never before been told in one place.

# Acknowledgements

In addition to thanking the staffs of each of the fourteen libraries and archives listed in the bibliography under Unpublished Sources—Original Sources, I would like to thank Nicholas Henderson for his excellent research at the William L. Clements Library, John K. Robertson for giving me access to some of his Rhode Island State Archives work and Bert Caudron for proofreading a draft of this book (his third book of mine, for which I am very grateful). I thank my son, Ryan McBurney, for building a website for my books and for his social media skills for history authors. I also express my deep appreciation to my wife, Margaret, for her support of my projects.

For the convenience of the reader, I have corrected spelling, grammar and punctuation in quoted material.

# 1
# Captain James Wallace Terrorizes Narragansett Bay
## April 1775 to April 1776

### Walter Chaloner's Spy Ring

In early 1774, Captain James Wallace, commander of the twenty-gun Royal Navy frigate *Rose*, went to work enforcing British maritime laws and capturing smugglers in Narragansett Bay. Once hostilities between the British and Americans broke out at Lexington and Concord on April 5, 1775, Wallace launched a yearlong campaign to intimidate Whigs and dampen their rebellious spirit. His ship—reinforced at times by the twenty-gun *Glasgow*, the sixteen-gun *Swan* and the ten-gun bomb brig *Bolton*—seized unsuspecting merchant ships as prizes; threatened to burn Newport to the ground (resulting in many of its citizens fleeing the port for the remainder of the war); bombarded the port of Bristol, to the north, until its citizens provided him with sheep; raided Jamestown, burning some fifteen houses and killing an eighty-year-old man; and plundered farms fronting the southern Rhode Island coast for their sheep and cattle. For his efforts to suppress the rebellion in Rhode Island, Wallace was later knighted by King George III.[1]

Wallace was aided in his work by a number of prominent area Loyalists, including men such as retired merchant Robert Ferguson. In 1750, Ferguson had moved from Scotland to Newport, where he engaged in the "Guinea Trade"—each year sending out a single ship to purchase slaves on the African coast and carry them across the Atlantic Ocean. After the end of the

Revolutionary War, in Ferguson's application for reimbursement of his war losses, Wallace informed the Royal Commission in London that Ferguson was "very loyal" and that he had "often received very useful intelligence of ye designs of ye rebels from" him and Captain James Keith.[2]

While Wallace terrorized Narragansett Bay from April 1775 to March 1776, a Continental army, ultimately commanded by George Washington, surrounded Boston and penned in British forces there. This led to two spectacular episodes of spying in Newport.

Walter Chaloner lost the office of sheriff of Newport County in 1774, after being elected to the post for seven years, due to his strong Tory sympathies and the increasing Whig influence. In 1786, he wrote down the story of his efforts to establish a spy ring designed both to keep Wallace apprised of the latest intelligence and to bring escaped Loyalists from and near Boston to safety on board one of Wallace's ships in Narragansett Bay. Assisting Chaloner were two trustworthy men, "one a bold, active white man by the name of [William] Crossing, formerly a deputy sheriff under him, and the other a black man." For almost a year, Crossing and the unnamed black man frequently ferried to Wallace Loyalists "who had made their escape out of Boston" and "who were obliged to seek shelter on board His Majesty's ships for the safety of their lives." "The danger attending the service being great," Crossing and his assistant "were obliged to perform the business on dark and stormy nights, in which they often suffered severe hardships."[3]

One trip led to the unraveling of Chaloner's spy ring. After carrying another group of Loyalists on a "stormy night" to the safety of the *Rose*, Crossing and the black man "went to the fireplace as usual to warm and dry themselves" on board Wallace's frigate. Earlier in the day, Wallace had captured a merchant vessel, and one of the men detained from it was then "by the fire and...knew Crossing." A few days later, after an unsuspecting Wallace released the man, he immediately notified Whig authorities of Crossing's being on board Wallace's ship. "Crossing, without suspicion of danger, was soon taken and strongly guarded" in a Newport jail.

The Sons of Liberty then became "wholly fixed" on Chaloner, knowing of his close relationship with Crossing. Chaloner further felt "extreme danger" from "the panic of the black for fear of being charged with being on board" the *Rose*. After calming the black man down, within several days, the enterprising Crossing escaped from his prison and found a place to hide. Patriot authorities twice searched Chaloner's home and placed "guards and sentinels...in all parts of the town to prevent" Crossing from escaping to one of Wallace's ships. Chaloner eventually discovered Crossing's hiding place

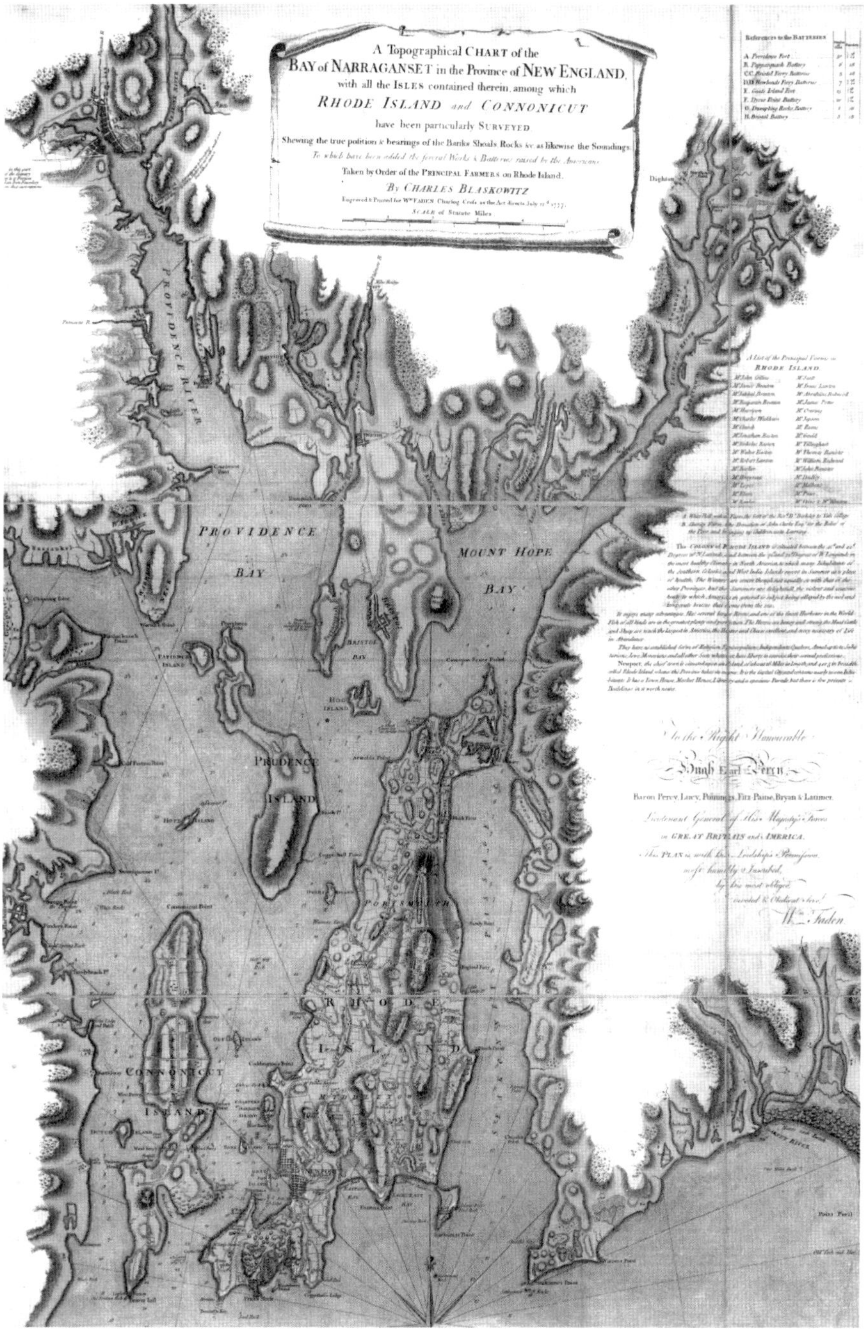


*A Topographical Chart of the Bay of Narragansett* by Charles Blaskowitz, London, 1777. *Library of Congress.*

The British frigate *Rose* took on board escaped Loyalists as well as spies. *Image of operational copy of the ship from John Fitzhugh Millar.*

(with the assistance of a second black man), but with all the boats in town secured by the guards each night, they could not find a way to get to a British warship anchored in Narragansett Bay.

Chaloner came up with an idea to escape from Newport. He found "a very long and wide plank" of wood that "was deemed sufficient to support his weight." Chaloner then took it into the shop of a local carpenter, whom Chaloner knew to be "a zealous friend" to the Crown. The former sheriff paid the carpenter to build a seat on the plank and have it ready for him at a moment's notice. Finally, one dark night when the wind was not too strong, Chaloner made his escape attempt. He had to paddle to the *Glasgow*, then two miles away. During the perilous journey, he "experienced very great danger and fatigue" and choppy water "overset his plank several times." Being "very strong" and determined not to die, after "several hours hard labor," he finally reached and boarded the *Glasgow*. Chaloner did not say what happened to Crossing or his black assistant, though it is known that Crossing later worked with Chaloner for the British army during its occupation of Newport.

## Mary Wenwood Mistakenly Trusts Her Former Husband

Perhaps the most infamous American spy to be detected, prior to Benedict Arnold, was traced and exposed due to the role of a Newport woman. Her name was Mary Wenwood, formerly Mary Butler, someone that Reverend Ezra Stiles of Newport's First Congregationalist Church referred to as "a girl of pleasure."[4] In July 1775, Wenwood travelled from Cambridge, Massachusetts, to ask her former husband, Godfrey Wenwood, who kept a bakery at Banister's wharf in Newport, to deliver a letter to Captain James Wallace of the *Rose*. If that were not possible, he was to deliver it to Charles Dudley, the Newport customs collector, or to George Rome, a renowned Loyalist then residing in Newport. Either of them, in turn, could make sure the letter reached Wallace, who could see it delivered to British authorities in occupied Boston.

Mary thought her divorced husband was a Loyalist and that she could trust him. In fact, he was contemplating marrying another local woman and recognized immediately the risk involved in delivering correspondence to Wallace, Dudley or Rome. He agreed to the task, but never completed it. Instead, he took the letter to his friend, Adam Maxwell, who ran a school in the front room of the nearby Brick Market. Together, they opened the letter, but were unable to read it because it was in code. At some point, Maxwell asked Reverend Stiles, a staunch Patriot, if he knew how to decipher characters, but apparently they never showed the minister the letter.[5]

Two months later, Godfrey Wenwood received a letter from his now-anxious ex-wife, who wondered why her "sister" had never received the letter. She wanted to know if Godfrey had sent it and whether "you ever got an answer from my sister."[6]

Godfrey immediately became apprehensive. Only a British supporter could have known that the letter had not reached British-held Boston. Further, the letter's author was likely an enemy to the Whig cause. He and Maxwell therefore travelled to Providence and showed the letter to Henry Ward, secretary of state in Rhode Island's Whig-controlled government. Ward sent the men on to Brigadier General Nathanael Greene, commander of the Rhode Island contingent of the Continental army then surrounding Boston. In his letter of introduction for the men, Ward advised Greene that "the strictest inquiry ought to be made."[7] After meeting with Wenwood and Maxwell in late September, Greene promptly forwarded both letters to the commander in chief of the Continental army, General Washington.

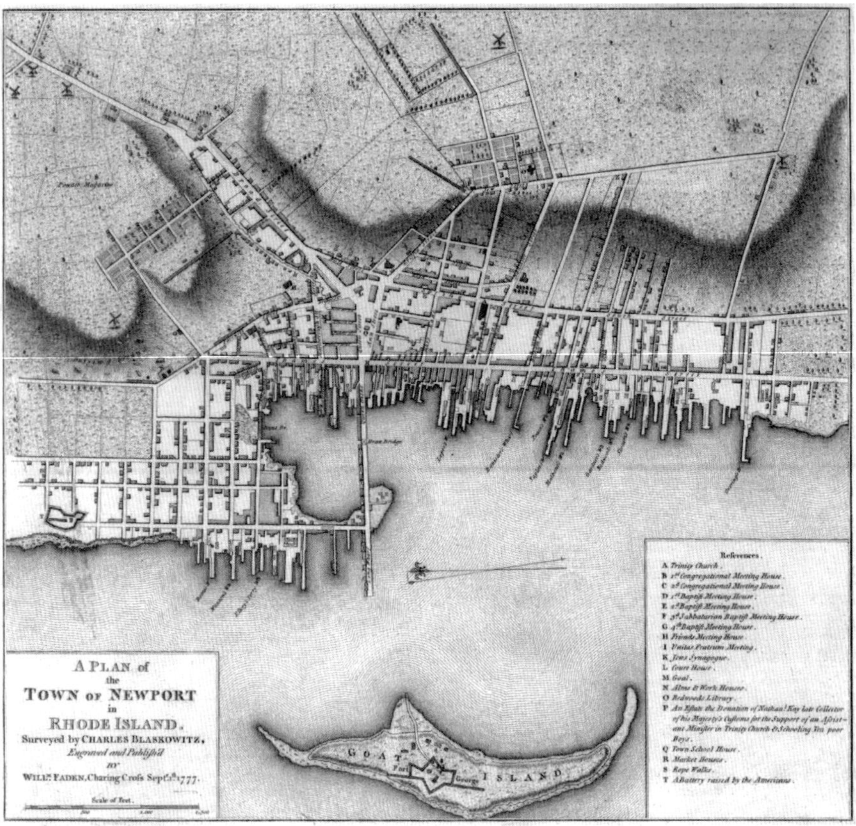


*A Plan of the Town of Newport in Rhode Island*, surveyed by Charles Blaskowitz, London, 1777. *Library of Congress.*

Greene's expedience paid off. "Realizing that the ciphered letter probably contained military intelligence and that a spy was most assuredly in their midst," wrote John Nagy in his recent, authoritative book, *Dr. Benjamin Church, Spy*, "Washington acted quickly. He sent Wenwood to meet with the woman (his ex-wife) to use the confidence she had in him to find out who had given her the letter. But she was not so easily fooled, and Wenwood's efforts were unsuccessful." Washington then ordered Mary Wenwood to headquarters. After being "terrified by the threats of severe punishment," she finally revealed that the author of the ciphered letter was Dr. Benjamin Church.[8]

The revelation shocked Patriots. Dr. Church was the grandson of a Little Compton native of the same name, a famous Indian fighter whose company had killed King Philip in 1676. Dr. Church was then serving as the surgeon general of the Continental army and, in that role, frequently met with General Washington. He was a sitting member of the Massachusetts Provincial Congress and, as a member of the Sons of Liberty, had worked closely with Whig leaders such as John and Samuel Adams and John Hancock.

Once the Americans deciphered the code used in his letter (according to Nagy, the code was not difficult to crack), Church's roles as a spy and traitor were confirmed. The letter, which Church had written in his Cambridge residence, was intended for Major Edward Crane of the British Forty-Third Regiment, then in Boston. It disclosed the strength of the Continental army, the state of its supplies and gunpowder and the number of artillery pieces the Americans had. Church also passed on prophetic advice for General Thomas Gage, the commander of British forces in Boston: "A view to independence grows more and more general. Should Britain declare war against the Colonies, they are lost forever." He concluded his letter with a request for Major Crane "to write me largely in cipher, by the way of Newport, addressed to Thomas Richards, merchant."[9] Church was arrested, jailed on orders of the Continental Congress and tried for and convicted of treason.[10] After spending about a year in jail, he was permitted to depart on a schooner for the Carribean. Neither ship nor doctor was ever heard from again.

It turned out that Mary Wenwood was Church's pregnant mistress. Unfortunately for Church, who had been increasing his coffers with payments from his British spymasters in Boston, she made the crucial mistake of trusting that her former husband would not betray her.

2

# The British Occupy Newport and the Rest of Aquidneck Island

## December 1776 to August 1777

### The British Invade—The First Spies

On December 8, 1776, Lieutenant General Henry Clinton and 7,100 British, Hessian and Tory troops, on board a fleet of seventy-one warships and transport vessels, seized Newport, Rhode Island, and the rest of Aquidneck Island. Patriot troops, no match for this overwhelming ground and sea force, evacuated the island, allowing Clinton's troops to land without resistance.

In short order, British forces occupied all of Aquidneck Island, just fourteen miles long and two miles wide, and small Conanicut Island, opposite Newport Harbor. His job quickly and easily completed, Clinton departed, leaving command of the British garrison to Lieutenant General Hugh Earl Percy. Percy's second in command was Major General Richard Prescott.

Commodore Sir Peter Parker, commanding British naval forces at Newport, immediately stationed frigates in the three entrances to Narragansett Bay, thus keeping privateers and commercial vessels from coming in and out of the bay. "I am very much pleased with the good news you have sent unto me, which secures an excellent port for the ships," King George III wrote to the Earl of Sandwich.[11]

Still, the British only occupied about one-quarter of Rhode Island. The rest of the state—and neighboring Bristol, Dartmouth and Plymouth

British warships in Narragansett Bay. They dispatched small boats filled with soldiers ready to occupy Newport and the rest of Aquidneck Island. *The Attack of Rhode Island, December 8th, 1776*, a watercolor by Irvan Bevan (1852–1940). *Mariners' Museum.*

"A Southwest View of Newport." Engraving from a painting by Samuel King, circa 1795. *Newport Historical Society.*

Counties in Massachusetts—were firmly in the Whig camp. This was confirmed by a Loyalist spy, who informed General Percy that in Providence, "the inhabitants are notorious rebels, scarcely a loyal subject to be found." East of Narragansett Bay, the spy found Bristol's inhabitants were "disloyal." In Taunton, Massachusetts, "a fine village," the inhabitants were all "rebels, except a few at Swansea called Quakers." It was the same throughout the rest of southeastern New England.[12]

In Providence, Major General Joseph Spencer of Haddam, Connecticut, assumed command of Patriot continental, state and militia forces in the Rhode Island theater of war. In March, Spencer received assistance from one of America's best generals, Major General Benedict Arnold.

As early as December 12, 1776, Clinton had at least two spies in the Rhode Island theater. He hoped that one would learn whether or not New England troops gathering in Providence, Bristol and Tiverton planned to assault Newport or simply defend against a British advance north.[13]

Clinton's spy network was expanded by his successor, General Percy. From his earliest correspondence, Percy received letters from Tories (some anonymous) in Rhode Island containing information on the topography of the theater: rivers that an army would have to cross, how deep the water was in various coastal areas and the Loyalist sympathies of the local residents.[14] On February 27, 1777, Percy received startlingly accurate information about Benedict Arnold's plan to assault Newport, including the numbers and locations of his troops, as well as his hopes of invading Aquidneck Island via Howland's Ferry, Bristol Ferry and Brenton Neck.[15]

Meeting with Lord Percy could be risky. In February 1778, Jonathan Lawton from Newport confessed to meeting with Percy, who asked him to persuade four persons in southern Rhode Island to promote enlistments in the regiment of Loyalists being organized by Colonel Edward Cole in Newport. Lawton agreed but was soon caught; he claimed that Cole forced him to cooperate with Percy.[16] Around the same time, inveterate Tory Ebenezer Slocum, from North Kingstown, admitted to twice crossing in a small

Lieutenant General Hugh Earl Percy. *Library of Congress.*

boat to Conanicut Island and then to Newport to meet with Percy.[17] After spending several months in dirty Providence jails, surprisingly, both Lawton and Slocum were found not guilty and were released.[18]

The British command took particular care to prevent American spies from entering British lines. In the February 6, 1777 edition of the Loyalist *Newport Gazette* appeared a proclamation, issued by Major General Richard

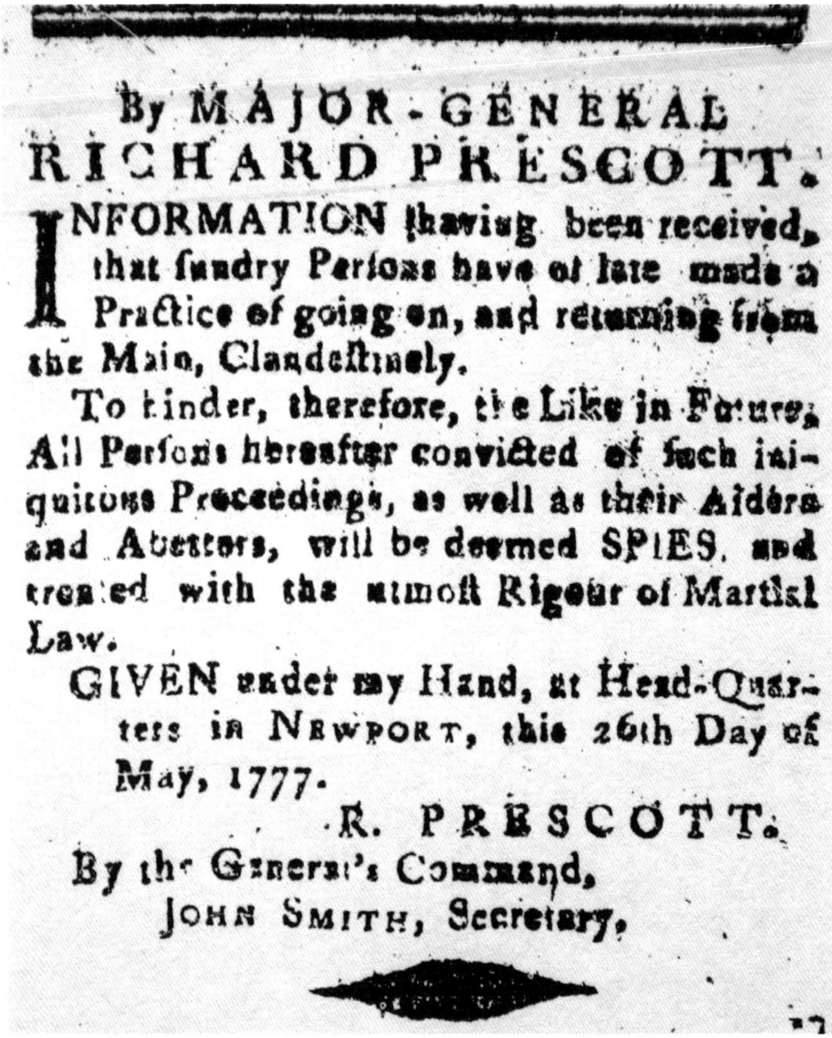

By MAJOR-GENERAL
RICHARD PRESCOTT.

INFORMATION having been received, that ſundry Perſons have of late made a Practice of going on, and returning from the Main, Clandeſtinely.

To hinder, therefore, the Like in Future, All Perſons hereafter convicted of ſuch iniquitous Proceedings, as well as their Aiders and Abettors, will be deemed SPIES, and treated with the utmoſt Rigour of Martial Law.

GIVEN under my Hand, at Head-Quarters in NEWPORT, this 26th Day of May, 1777.

R. PRESCOTT.

By the General's Command,
JOHN SMITH, Secretary.

Proclamation issued by Major General Richard Prescott warning any civilians that, if caught traveling to or from the mainland without permission, they would be treated as "SPIES." *Newport Gazette, May 29, 1777.*

Major General Richard Prescott. *New England Magazine, Sept. 1894.*

Prescott, directing "all strangers coming into this town or neighborhood" to present themselves to him or his deputy, and that "no inhabitant is…to receive any [such] person into his house, without immediately reporting him…on pain of military execution." On May 29, 1777, the newspaper printed another missive from Prescott (now in command in Newport) warning civilians that "all persons" caught traveling to and from the mainland "clandestinely," as well as their "aiders and abettors," would be treated as "SPIES" and be subject to "the utmost rigor of martial law"—with the clear implication that the punishment would be death.

In September 1777, the British discovered that some daring Rhode Islanders, probably based in Little Compton, "have made a practice of coming over during the night in a boat, which they sunk near the beach to prevent her being discovered; that they have then gone into Newport, where they have purchased rum and salt, and the following night returned to the shore, weighed their boat and crossed the Sakonnet River again." Major Frederick Mackenzie, who monitored espionage activities for the British in Newport, added that "there is no doubt these persons have come for the purpose of gaining intelligence, which is not difficult to be obtained, as the majority of inhabitants are friends [i.e., Whigs]."[19]

The British went so far as to put in a Newport jail a nearly ninety-year-old Jamestown man, Daniel Weedon, who was accused of "hoisting signals" to the Americans.[20] A Newport resident was seen merely watching an American vessel in the distance and was also committed to the Newport jail.[21]

If a spy "in disguise" (non-military, civilian dress) was caught behind enemy lines, the protocol of the day required that he be put to death by hanging. There is no record that the British in Newport ever hung an

American for being a spy, but the risk was always there. Certainly, that risk did not stop brave men from taking their chances. In late February 1778, for example, some Americans in Tiverton obtained, probably from a British army deserter, the British "countersigns," the passwords that had to be used when hailed by guards. They then snuck onto Aquidneck Island and learned that some British troops were under orders to be ready to sail to Philadelphia by March 20. This information was passed along to a Massachusetts state legislator, who in turn sent it to General Washington at Valley Forge.[22]

## John Trevett Risks His Life for an Afternoon's Spying

The American who probably came closest to being caught and hanged as a spy in Newport was Lieutenant John Trevett of the Continental navy sloop *Providence*. Born in Newport in 1747, Trevett had worked as a crew member on merchant ships sailing out of the port. On January 17, 1777, Trevett went on board a "flag" vessel commanded by Captain John Ayres of Boston, who had permission for his ship to enter Newport Harbor in order to pick up Massachusetts prisoners as part of a prisoner exchange. Swapping prisoners was one of the only times during the British blockade that American vessels were allowed to enter Newport Harbor.

Once he learned of his assignment to accompany Ayres to Newport, Trevett hatched a daring, borderline reckless plan to gain intelligence. Prior to his departure, he dressed as an ordinary sailor and let his beard grow, in hopes that he would not be recognized in his hometown. After Ayres's vessel sailed from Providence and docked near the Long Wharf in Newport, Trevett persuaded a British officer that he needed to obtain some fresh water nearby. Instead, he walked into the heart of downtown Newport, amid British troops and well-known Tories strolling the streets.

Trevett made his way to the tavern (still standing today at 111 Clarke Street) operated by Peleg Barker, whom he knew to be a Patriot sympathizer. The tavern was then being used as the quarters of the top Hessian officers, and Hessian sentries stood at its front door. Trevett therefore snuck inside through the back kitchen door. The adventurous lieutenant then eased into a room, where he found Barker and Deacon Peckham of Middletown. Trevett asked the astonished and frightened Barker and Peckham to disclose "useful information about the condition of the occupying troops and where they were stationed on

Aquidneck Island." On receiving this information, Trevett then made his way to Captain Lillibridge's tavern on the parade ground next to the Court House (the Old Colony House), where he ordered a drink in a room crowded with British and Hessian officers. Lillibridge, who Trevett knew to dislike the British, "could not help shedding tears for my safety." Trevett then spotted an acquaintance of his, the notorious Tory William Crossing, out on the street, about to enter the tavern through the door to the very room where he was. Trevett quickly slipped out another door onto a side street, avoiding Crossing. He had another close call soon after when the wealthy Tory merchant John Wanton recognized Trevett and called out his name. Wary now, Trevett ignored him and made his way safely back onto Captain Ayres's vessel.

The next day, after taking on board forty-eight suffering American prisoners, Ayres pulled his vessel out of Newport and sailed back to Providence. Trevett later reported his intelligence findings to his superiors in Providence.[23]

## The Hanging of John Hart, Spy

In British-controlled New York City, the printing of counterfeit American money for use by certain Loyalists received official British sanction. The purpose was both to help Loyalists pay their taxes and to get the fake money into general circulation. That, presumably, would lessen confidence in American currency, which would in turn undermine the American economy and war effort. The organizers of the scheme were so bold that on April 14, 1777, they placed an advertisement in the *New York Gazette* seeking persons to carry "into other colonies…any number of counterfeit Congress notes."[24] In an April 18 letter to Congress, General Washington enclosed a copy of the advertisement, writing that the scheme "shows that no artifices are left untried by the enemy to injure us."[25]

As part of the British plan, John Hart had arrived in Newport in January 1777 with a letter of introduction from William Tryon, a prominent Loyalist and former governor of New York. Tryon described Hart for Percy's benefit: he was in his mid-forties, about five feet, five inches tall, strong limbed, with a fresh complexion. In March, Tryon wrote a follow-up letter thanking Percy for assisting Hart.[26]

British secret service authorities in New York City had persuaded Hart to carry counterfeit notes to Rhode Island and distribute them to Loyalists.

Hart was later described in the Patriot press as hailing from the New York locale of "Otter Creek," which the author has not identified.[27] However, former Newport pastor Ezra Stiles, a reliable source who had fled Newport for nearby Dighton, Massachusetts, indicated that Hart had been born in Little Compton, Rhode Island.[28] The 1774 census lists a Jonathan Hart in

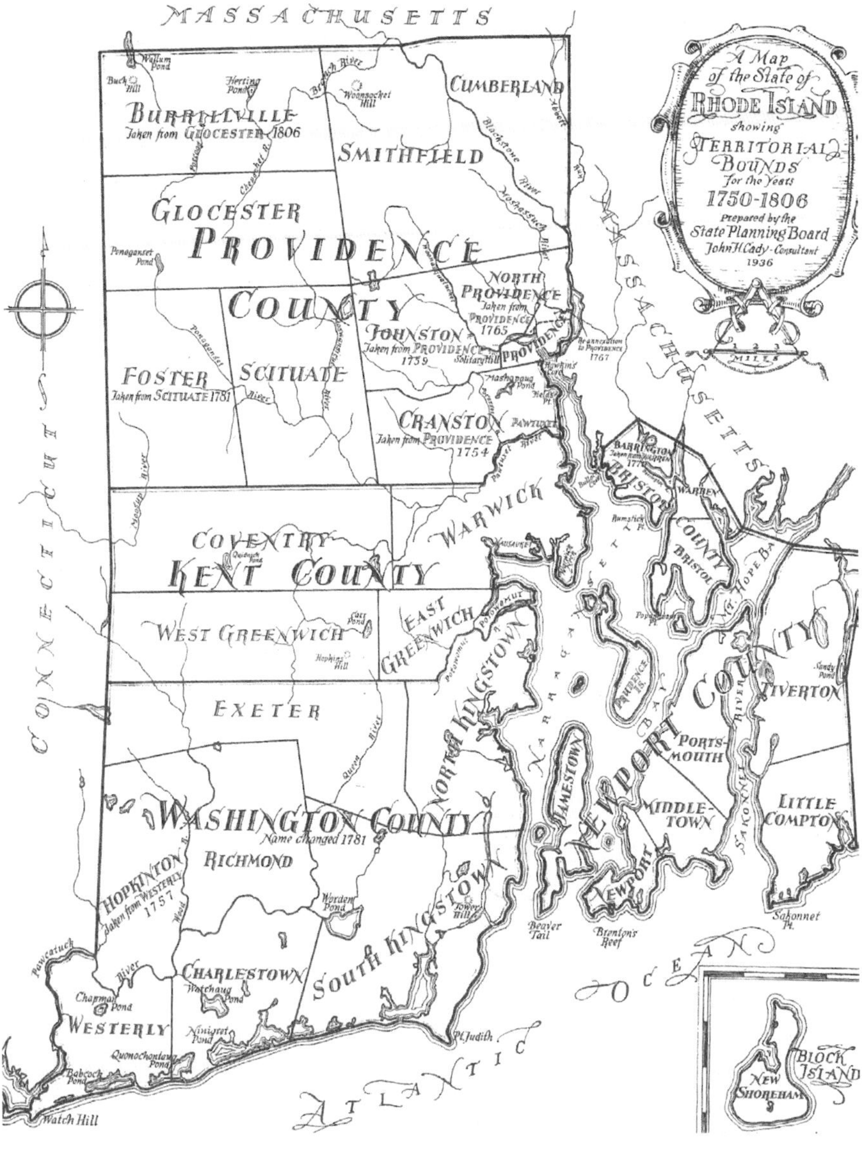


Map of Rhode Island, 1750–1806. *John Hutchins Cady, Rhode Island Boundaries, 1636–1936.*

Little Compton, with a wife and three young children; he could have been the spy.[29]

From January through April 1777, John Hart performed secret services on the Rhode Island mainland to encourage Loyalists to escape to Newport and enlist in Loyalist regiments being raised there. Hart, now armed with fake Massachusetts money, distributed it to local Loyalists, such as the Slocum family in North Kingstown.

General Percy thought enough of Hart's efforts to mention them in his military diary. For February 10, the British commander in chief wrote, "Mr. Hart returned this night" from the mainland to Aquidneck Island. Two days later, Percy recorded that Hart and another Loyalist crossed Narragansett Bay "to the Narragansett shore" where "they promise to bring over men and cattle, etc." The Tory raiders also expressed a "desire to burn the rebel magazine." Percy next mentioned Hart in his entry for February 27: "Hart came back again and set out again in the evening," presumably back to the mainland in southern Rhode Island. After spending more time in enemy territory, Hart returned on March 4, this time with Charles Slocum, brother of Ebenezer Slocum.[30]

By April, Hart had grown bolder. On April 11, Percy wrote that Hart and two other men "went off this night to seize, if possible, some of the Assembly and bring them off" the mainland to Aquidneck Island. At the time, the state legislature was in session in Little Rest (now Kingston) in South Kingstown. Hart, thus, wanted to kidnap a few members of the General Assembly and have them thrown in a Newport prison.

Once in North Kingstown, Hart and his Tory friends altered their mission to capture George Waite Babcock of Updike's Newtown (present-day Wickford). Babcock, a firm Patriot, had formed an independent company called the Newtown Rangers, with the main task of hunting local Tories. In April, Babcock became the unit's first commander, with the rank of captain.[31] With the assistance of four sailors from Royal Navy warships in Narragansett Bay, Hart made an attempt, according to Percy, "to seize Babcock in Updike's Newtown, but he [Babcock] escaped. They drove the [Patriot] guards, however, and returned back here without anybody hurt."[32]

Unfortunately for Hart, his luck was about to run out. An unidentified Continental officer, while a prisoner in New York City, had learned of Hart's plan to carry counterfeit money into New England. On his release in early April 1777, this officer provided that information to Washington. On April 12, Washington wrote to Governor Jonathan Trumbull of Connecticut, naming Hart specifically and requesting Trumbull to pass the information along so that Hart could be "detected and apprehended."[33]

Brigadier General James Mitchell Varnum. *History of the State of Rhode Island.*

While Hart was on another assignment in southern Rhode Island, Patriot authorities were alerted to his plans, and militia began searching for him and other Tories. The *Newport Gazette* reported that George Waite Babcock and his Newtown Rangers were going "from town to town, upon the Narragansett shore…taking up all persons who are suspected of being friendly to the" Crown.[34]

Feeling the heat, Hart arranged for the HMS *Orpheus*, stationed off North Kingstown's shore, to pick him up. Near midnight on May 12, a small British party landed near Quidnessett, in North Kingstown, to find and take off the mainland a "spy," who presumably was Hart. But the interlopers were spotted. A British midshipman on the mission, Bartholomew James, recalled, "We advanced within a few yards of the beach, when, the coast being alarmed, the rebels began a heavy fire at us, and had nearly cut off our retreat, but through great good fortune we escaped with a few shot only striking the boat."[35] Hart was on his own.

Early on Tuesday, May 13, Brigadier General James Varnum and Colonel Henry Sherburne (both Rhode Islanders), with the assistance of county militia units and the independent Newtown Rangers, intensified their search for Hart. Seventeen-year-old Wanton Casey of East Greenwich was known to keep a "fleet horse" and was asked to join the search party. He later recalled: "I well remember going out one night, under the command of General Varnum and Colonel Sherburne, in search of a man named Hart (a spy from the enemy), and after riding all night, and taking some suspected persons, who informed us where to find him, we surrounded a house in Exeter, just at daylight, and after searching sometime we found where he was secreted."[36] The key to the search was grabbing Tory suspects and intimidating them into divulging information about Hart's whereabouts. Varnum and his party found in Hart's possession a number of counterfeit Massachusetts bills. Hart's days as a spy were over.

On Friday, May 16, Hart was examined in Providence by the Rhode Island Council of War. The council concluded that Hart should be tried as a spy in a military court and recommended that Major General Spencer establish a court martial to try him.[37] By not being put on trial in a civil court as a counterfeiter, and instead being put on trial as a spy in a military court, Hart was more likely to receive a death sentence.

Spencer agreed to try Hart in a military court. Remarkably, it appears that Hart was tried by a military tribunal in Providence that same day. In the court-martial proceeding, Hart admitted to distributing the phony money. He also confessed to "giving intelligence" to British commanders in Newport and assisting in the recruitment of Tory regiments. Moreover, he "openly approved of the King's cause & wished success to it."[38] Predictably, the court-martial board convicted Hart and sentenced him to death.

While chained to the wall in his jail cell, Hart likely thought about the fate of other spies in similar circumstances. He must have realized that he was not the only Loyalist in New England in his shoes. When he was caught behind American lines a few months earlier, a Tory named Moses Dunbar held a British army commission to enlist soldiers in Tory regiments. On March 19, 1777, after a brief trial, Dunbar was convicted of treason by a court martial and hanged on a hill outside Hartford, the first Tory to be executed in Connecticut.[39]

Later in March, in New London, a Loyalist named Jethro Beebe heard about Dunbar's execution—news that, to him, was "enough to make a Christian's heart ache." Beebe reported the gruesome rumor of the details of Dunbar's botched hanging:

> [Dunbar] *was carried to the place of execution and when they drove the cart from under him the knot did not slip. This brought the knot up against his chin and it neither choked him nor broke his neck. Then he strove so as to clear his hands and take hold of the rope. They then took hold of his legs and pulled him down in order to kill him that way. This stretched the rope so as to bring his feet to touch the ground and then they dug away the ground under his feet and let him hang about 50 minutes and then cut him down. It was declared by some that he was not dead when they cut him down. But they buried him in a grave where there was water and he is said have drowned after all.*[40]

Hart could only hope that he would be pardoned by General Spencer or, at least, that his execution would be more humane.

Two Tories who were captured in Danbury, Connecticut, with more than $10,000 in counterfeit bills in their possession were also executed in Hartford. Still another who was caught recruiting Tory soldiers was hung in Hartford on May 29, 1777.[41] Of course, on the American side, Patriots remembered Connecticut's Nathan Hale, who was hung as a spy by General William Howe's order on September 22, 1776, after his famous words regretting that he had but one life to lose for his country.

The day after Hart's sentencing, the gallows for his execution was built. Later the same day, the convicted spy was guided out of his jail and delivered to it. After what the *Newport Gazette* called a "short but pathetic speech," Hart was summarily hanged.[42] Reverend Ezra Stiles accurately observed in his diary that this was indeed "speedy justice."[43] Hart reportedly left a wife and several children.[44] He had the unlucky distinction of being one of only a handful of persons ever hanged by government authorities in Rhode Island.

3

# *Spencer's Expedition*

# September 1777 to April 1778

## Isaac Goodman: Britain's Invaluable Spy

The most spectacular intelligence coup during the British occupation of Newport occurred during Spencer's Expedition, in October of 1777. At the time, New England officials were making plans and gathering troops to invade Aquidneck Island and move against the British garrison in Newport. Without any Continental troops to support inexperienced militia, surprise was of the essence. The planned expedition was named after the commander in chief of the American army in the Rhode Island theater, Major General Joseph Spencer.

Great lengths were taken to keep the invasion plans from the British. Even newspapers kept mum about troop movements. Calls for troops were made in late September; those who answered were directed to be in Tiverton by early October, which would leave deserters little time to warn the enemy. New Englanders were naturally aware of the troop buildup, but they did not know its purpose: an invasion of Aquidneck Island by an eight-thousand-man force. For a long time, efforts to keep the invasion plans secret from British commanders were remarkably successful.

The British did begin to receive hints of a possible invasion from spies and Tories. On September 3, 1777, four Tories who had fled from Cape Cod entered Newport with information that "great preparations" were being made to attack Aquidneck Island.[45] Major Frederick Mackenzie, in his diary entry for September 17, 1777, noted: "Information has been received that the rebels are collecting a great number of boats at Providence, preparatory to their making an attack upon this island."[46] On September 29, 1777, eight Tories, seeking to evade the draft of most able-bodied men into the militia, escaped from southeastern Massachusetts in a sloop, arrived at Newport and informed their British interrogators that the draft was for an American invasion of Aquidneck Island. But the British did not believe it. At the time, the great theater of war was in northern New York, where General John Burgoyne was attempting to march his army from Canada to Albany. The British thought that the draft was to reinforce General Horatio Gates's army, which was opposing Burgoyne, a stroke of luck for the planners of Spencer's Expedition.[47]

Despite increasing signs of activity among New England troops in Tiverton, on October 16, 627 British troops from the Forty-Third Regiment and detachments from the Fifty-Fourth Regiment boarded transport ships for a raid on nearby Bedford (now New Bedford) and Fairhaven, Massachusetts. On October 9, five Tories from Sandwich, Massachusetts, who claimed to have been drafted against their will, had deserted to the British in Newport and informed their questioners that the gathering soldiers were indeed bound for General Gates's army in upstate New York. This confirmed British suspicions. The deserters also stated that the Bedford and Fairhaven harbors contained numerous privateers and commercial ships, as well as wharves full of stores. Based on this intelligence, the new commander in chief of the British garrison in Newport, Major General Robert Pigot, and the top Royal Navy commander at Newport, Admiral Sir Peter Parker, planned to raid the harbors and burn their contents. Pigot also made preparations to send to Long Island some ships carrying men to cut and carry wood back to Newport, which was desperately needed by his troops for the oncoming winter. Thus, while more than 8,000 American troops were on the brink of assaulting Aquidneck Island, the unsuspecting British, with only about 3,600 defenders, were on the verge of dispatching one-sixth of their entire force on comparatively meaningless expeditions.[48] This was an instance in which inaccurate intelligence from Loyalist civilian sources in the Rhode Island theater could have seriously damaged the British war effort.

A Newport native named Isaac Goodman saved the British at the last minute. A member of Newport's Jewish community, Goodman had emigrated from Germany in 1774 and sought work as a physician. He

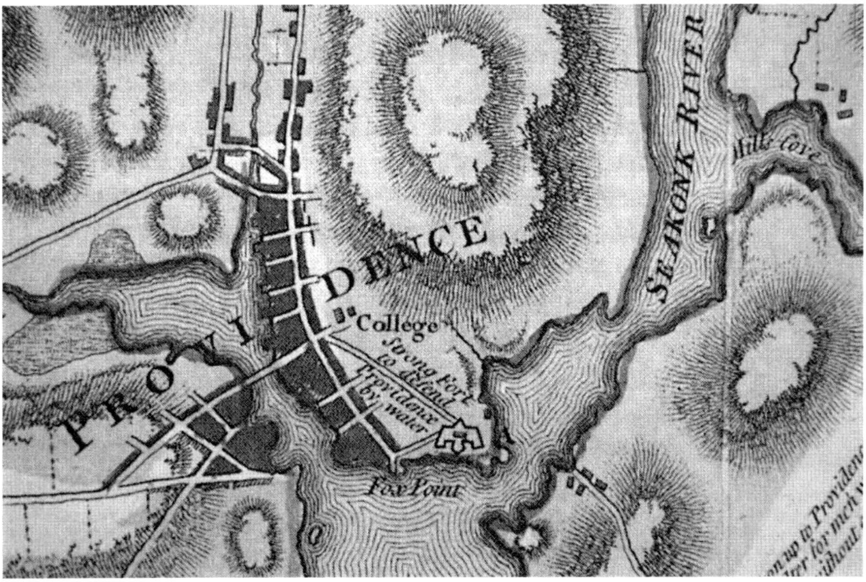


Providence area, detail from *A Topographical Chart of the Bay of Narragansett* by Charles Blaskowitz, London, 1777. *Library of Congress.*

apparently did not reside in his new home long enough to be infused with the increasing rebellious spirit infecting many Newporters. After the British occupation, he agreed to perform secret services for General Percy. In March 1777, Percy sent Goodman north to Providence with the mission to discover the Americans' next plans. Unfortunately for Goodman, whose heavy German accent no doubt made him stand out, he was almost immediately jailed on suspicion of being a Tory. He spent the next three months incarcerated, much of the time secured by iron cuffs, but when nobody appeared in court to testify against him at his hearing on June 5, he was released. Rather than head back to Newport immediately, Goodman remained on mainland Rhode Island for the following four months to complete his mission and gather what information he could.[49]

Goodman proved adept at such work, and sniffed out details of Spencer's Expedition. Based on the accurate information he later revealed to British officers, he must have either befriended or overheard a talkative American officer, perhaps even a general or a highly placed government official. He also probably frequented local taverns, which were always a good source of news.

Goodman finally decided to sneak back onto Aquidneck Island, which he did from Bristol Neck on the evening of October 16. British guards must not have believed he was actually a British informant with valuable information, as it was not until 1:00 a.m. on October 17 that Goodman finally met with General Pigot. The Tory informed Pigot of virtually every material detail involving Spencer's Expedition, including the number of troops and boats involved, the planned three-pronged attack from the Tiverton and Little Compton shores and the end-of-the-month expiration date of the militia's term of service.[50]

The British no doubt marveled at their good fortune. As a result of Goodman's information, Pigot immediately called off the twin expeditions and ordered the 627 troops back onto shore to beef up British defenses.[51] If the convoys had departed as planned, Pigot would have lost the services of a good portion of his soldiers, and Parker the use of two frigates and the sloop *Kingsfisher*, which operated in the shallow Sakonnet River. British and Hessian troops were placed on high alert, and on the night of October 19, British artillery batteries fired at American boats in the Sakonnet River, killing one soldier and disrupting the planned invasion—which had been scheduled to begin that night. As Major Mackenzie of the British army crassly put it, "It certainly was a very fortunate circumstance that the Jew came in at the time he did."[52]

The British then benefited from another source of intelligence: escaped prisoners. A British sailor from the HMS *Fox*, who had been captured by the Americans and pressed into service on a Rhode Island galley, escaped. He informed his superiors that the Americans had indeed planned to land on Aquidneck Island on the night of October 19 and that subsequent attempts to invade had been spoiled by bad weather. The following day, by which time Spencer's Expedition had been scrapped, two American deserters confirmed as much for British commanders. New England militiamen were returning to their homes.[53]

Not infrequently, historians exaggerate the importance of particular spies. Isaac Goodman's role in exposing New England plans to invade Aquidneck Island and retake Newport does not fall into that category. It was a spectacular intelligence coup for the British and justified their efforts to build a spy network on the Rhode Island mainland.

## The Taggarts: Father and Son Patriot Spies

During the planning stages of the ill-fated Spencer's Expedition, American commanders got information about British, Hessian and Tory troops from their own spy. His name was William Taggart, and he employed as a courier his son, William Taggart Jr.

Shortly after the British occupation of Newport in December 1776, a Hessian colonel moved into a substantial house in Middletown, almost five miles east of Newport's wharves off Howland Avenue and to the north of what is now Third Beach. The house's owner, forty-three-year-old William Taggart Sr., kept quiet about his own Whig sympathies. Taggart's wife, daughters and twenty-one-year-old son William Taggart Jr. cared little for their uninvited guest or the British occupation and departed for Little Compton, but William Taggart Sr. and two of his adult sons remained to watch over the family's thriving farm.

In about September 1777, the elder Taggart decided to become a spy for the American cause. Shortly before the troops began to gather for the planned Spencer's Expedition, he managed to pass a message to William Taggart Jr. that he wanted to see him. For young William, this meant slipping back onto the island and making his way to his home, avoiding British guards along the way. William Jr., who had not yet enlisted in the army, asked the commander of American forces at Tiverton, Colonel Joseph Stanton of the First Rhode Island State Regiment, for permission to visit his father. Stanton agreed, but he wanted experienced officers to hear William's father's report firsthand. Stanton sent three men with Taggart, including Lieutenant Charles Handy of Colonel Stanton's own regiment.

At night, the four Rhode Islanders secretly made their way by boat from the Little Compton shores across the Sakonnet River to the eastern shore of Middletown and skulked their way to William Taggart Sr.'s house on the opposite (western) side of the island. William Sr. then conveyed to them intelligence about the British military in Aquidneck Island, including troop strength, the positions of every regiment, the fact that the soldiers had dug few entrenchments and that the Royal Navy's strength was not particularly strong at that time. This information was passed to American commanders, who were emboldened by the intelligence and continued their plans for their secret expedition.

William Taggart Jr. subsequently made this secret trek home a habit, delivering messages from his father to Colonel Joseph Stanton at Howland's Ferry.[54] It was dangerous, but rewarding, work. On October 16, his father passed to the son "an exact return" of the troop strength of three regiments—two Hessian and one British—that he had cleverly obtained from a Hessian sergeant major. The information was immediately forwarded to the commander of the proposed expedition, General Spencer, who expressed his gratitude for the intelligence.[55]

William Taggart Sr. acquired information from a variety of sources, including the Hessian colonel living in his own house. In addition, Taggart asked an African American man, Cudjo, to keep his ears open for useful intelligence. Cudjo was aware that the Hessian colonel frequented the Marquis of Granby tavern, near the Old Colony House in Newport. And he knew a German-speaking woman employed there; she had been brought to Newport with her father aboard a Tory privateer. The woman, Gertrude Hegel, regularly listened to Hessian officers discussing military business in their native language. Cudjo made a point of regularly chatting with Gertrude, who sometimes repeated to Cudjo what she heard the officers say. She did so unwittingly, probably trying to impress him and unaware that he was a spy. From Cudjo, the information was passed to William Taggart Sr., who passed it to his son, who then forwarded it to American commanders on the mainland.[56]

British spy Isaac Goodman once nearly uncovered William Taggart Sr.'s secret work. At his crucial meeting with General Pigot in the early morning of October 17, Goodman stated that the Americans "have exact intelligence of everything doing on the island, and that some rebels were lately at the house of a person who conveys information to them."[57] Goodman must have had contacts with a loose-lipped, high-ranking Rhode Island military or civilian official to gain such secret information. Fortunately for the Taggarts, Goodman did not know the American spy's name nor the house that was visited.

By the night of October 19, the men gathered for Spencer's Expedition were ready. That night, an advance party for one of the army's three wings, consisting of William Taggart Jr. and about thirty soldiers from Colonel Stanton's regiment, crossed the Sakonnet River to a spot below Black Point. William Taggart Jr. then made his way to the Taggart house, picked up his father and two brothers and took them to Black Point. There, the Taggarts and soldiers of the advance party waited for the signal indicating that the Patriot landing force was heading toward them. Meanwhile, they spotted a sergeant and a private of the British Seventeenth Regiment of the Light Dragoons patrolling by horseback along a road. They faced a quandary. If they captured these men, it might give away the entire American plan. Despite the risk, they took both men prisoner.[58]

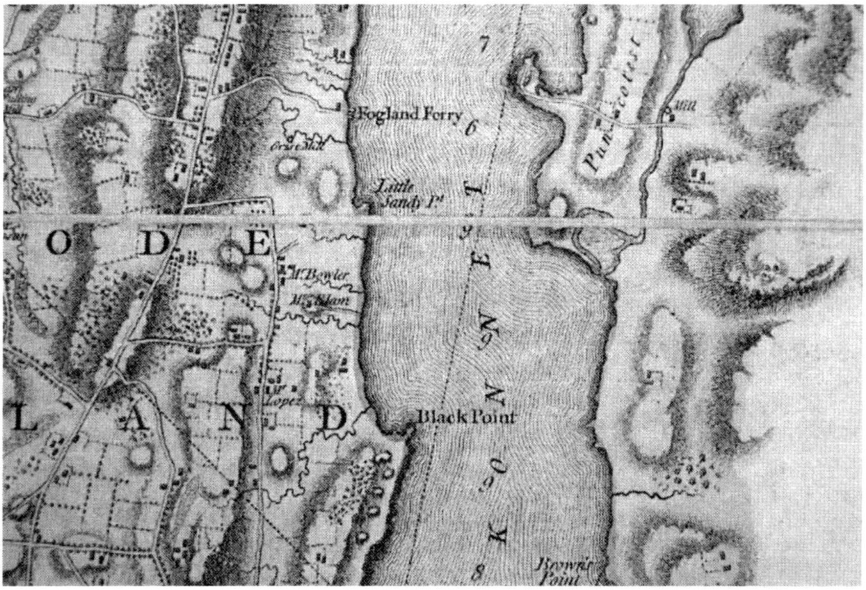


This map shows the area of spying operations of the Taggarts in Middletown and the surrounding area. Detail from *A Topographical Chart of the Bay of Narragansett* by Charles Blaskowitz, London, 1777. *Library of Congress.*

The efforts of the Taggarts and the rest of the Little Compton advance party went for naught, as Spencer cancelled the attack. Profoundly disappointed, the entire group returned to Little Compton with their two British captives. It was a particularly bitter time for the Taggarts, who had hoped that New England soldiers would retake Aquidneck Island. William Taggart Sr. immediately reported to General Spencer and expressed regret that by capturing the two dragoons, they had given away the Americans' intended landing place. Taggart also lamented his own situation: with the expedition called off, his considerable estate was at risk.[59] The fate of Cudjo is unknown.

William Taggart Sr. paid a heavy price for his work as a Patriot spy. When the British discovered his role, General Pigot ordered the Taggarts' livestock and corn seized and permitted vengeful Hessian soldiers to plunder and pull down his fine house and all of his farm buildings and to burn his orchards. British troops left nothing on the farm but dirt.[60]

## THE ONE-LEGGED SPY

It was not only Rhode Island Patriot authorities who worried about Tories supplying the Newport garrison and escaping to Newport to join Loyalist bands of troops. Whig leaders in southeastern Massachusetts had to address the problem as well.

In March of 1778, a "one-legged stranger," as Edward Davis was called by locals, arrived in and visited Sandwich and other Barnstable County towns in southeastern Massachusetts. Consorting openly with Crown sympathizers, he claimed that he was from Providence and that his business was to change silver money for paper. Before long, local authorities threw him into a Plymouth jail.

The local committee of correspondence was responsible for investigating reports of Tory activities. Led by Nathaniel Freeman, it began interrogating men and women who had conversed with and assisted Davis. Ultimately, some fifty-five depositions were taken in March and April of 1778.

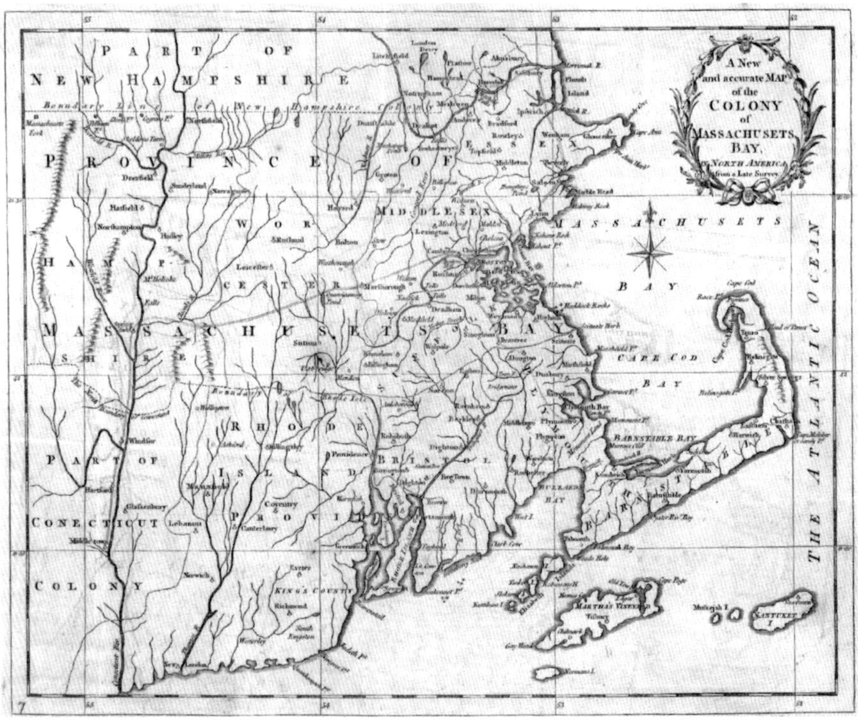


A map of southeastern New England, including Barnstable County, Massachusetts, encompassing the Cape Cod peninsula. J. Hinton, London, 1780. *Library of Congress.*

Those interrogated began pointing fingers, alerting Whig authorities to a nest of Tory sympathizers in their midst. Ebenezer Raymond was heard to say that he would have escaped to Rhode Island long ago if not for his wife and child. Josiah Goodspeed and Davis were spotted compiling a list of the chief men of Barnstable County (with Freeman and Brigadier General Joseph Otis at their head), apparently with the object of delivering the list to General Pigot in Newport.

The confessions continued. Seth Perry admitted that Davis had given him a stack of counterfeit bills "as thick as a stack of cards" and that Perry had burned them before he was hauled off to jail with Davis. Another man stated that Major Thomas Bourne had tried to convince him not to serve in the militia if he was drafted, and there was testimony that Bourne had expressed a desire to escape to Newport. The accusations continued, and a number of men were jailed as dangerous persons likely to assist "the enemy" in Newport. Someone then set fire to the Plymouth jailhouse, presumably in an effort to free Davis, Perry and other accused Tories.[61]

It turned out that one-legged Edward Davis was not a Tory at all, but a Patriot spy. Davis had been approached by a staunch Loyalist, Simon Cain of Mansfield in Worcester County. Cain wanted to help Loyalist volunteers get to Newport and for fellow sympathizers to supply provisions to the British garrison there. He also wanted Davis to spread counterfeit money among the inhabitants, as a way to financially assist Loyalists and, at the same time, to undermine the local economy. Davis agreed to carry Cain's written messages in his "hollow cane" and deliver them to General Pigot. But rather than cooperate with Cain, Davis brought the information to Whig leaders Major General William Heath and John Hancock in Boston. Heath and Hancock encouraged Davis to cooperate with Cain in order to root out Tory sympathizers. They provided him with a horse from the Continental army depot and sent him on his way to Barnstable County.[62]

Some of the incarcerated Loyalists in Barnstable did, in fact, make their way to Newport and support the Crown's cause. For example, Seth Perry broke out of a Barnstable County jail and fled to Newport, where he served as a guide for Royal Navy warships. Seth joined his brother Thomas, who had been one of the Tories who had fled to Newport to evade the draft for Spencer's Expedition and had informed British authorities of it. After that, Thomas Perry, according to his Loyalist claim, was "frequently employed by General Pigot to go into the interior parts of the country as a spy, and to procure intelligence, and several times was near being taken and his life in constant danger."[63]

The British on Aquidneck Island also once sent spies to test the loyalty of the surrounding populace. On the night of March 24, 1778, a small party of soldiers in Wightman's Regiment of Rhode Island Loyalists "disguised themselves" as Patriot militiamen "and pretended to have just come over from the eastern shore" of Little Compton. They then sought assistance from nearby Middletown inhabitants, who were happy to take them in. Wightman's men, to their chagrin, "discovered that nothing but the dread of The King's troops prevents the greatest part of the inhabitants from joining the rebels…" One of the hosts even "acknowledged that he was to have set fire to the hay magazine" that was closely guarded by the British in Newport. The next day, three of the inhabitants were jailed by order of General Pigot.[64]

4

# The Rhode Island Campaign

## May to September 1778

### Raids on Bristol and Warren, and Richard Holland

In early May 1778, General Pigot received reports from Loyalist spies and escaped British soldiers that Sullivan was collecting troops at Providence.[65] On May 2, the top German general in Newport, Frederick von Lossberg, wrote, "According to reports from the spies, the rebels are concentrating their strength in New England."[66] Aware that France had signed a treaty of alliance with the fledgling United States and could send a fleet of warships to North America, British leaders were rightly concerned about attacks on British-held garrisons.

From reports of spies, including from one sent out by Walter Chaloner, Pigot learned that the Americans had gathered about one hundred flatboats at a bridge spanning the Kickemuit River, near Warren, to be used in a major invasion of Aquidneck Island. He was also informed that the Americans had only 10 soldiers guarding the boats and not more than 250 troops on the peninsula from Warren to Bristol Ferry. Pigot's spies further discovered the location of military stores in Warren.[67]

The British mistakenly concluded that an assault on Newport was imminent. "The rebels are certainly preparing for an attack on this island," Major Mackenzie wrote confidently on May 22.[68] A Newport gentleman claimed that the Americans "were collecting a large force, and making great preparations in order to attack" Aquidneck Island.[69] Two days later, a rumor circulated in Newport that "the Provincials are about to attack the island with 2,000 men."[70] Why 2,000 Americans would invade an island

Major General John Sullivan. *Author's Collection.*

with 3,500 well-trained soldiers, supported by superior British naval forces, was not clear.

Actually, while the new American commander of the Rhode Island theater, Major General John Sullivan, hoped to launch such an offensive in the future with the assistance of the French, he was far from ready to be able to do so. The boats stored at Kickemuit River were left over from Spencer's Expedition, and, for the moment, were merely being repaired.

The misleading reports that Pigot received from his spies spurred him to action. Around May 22, Pigot met with the ranking officer of the British navy in Newport, Captain Walter Griffith, and decided the time was ripe for a raid on Warren and Bristol. By destroying the Americans' boats and military stores, Pigot expected to delay the anticipated American advance. He was confident the "whole business" could be "finished" before the Americans could assemble a significant force for a counterattack.[71]

The raid commenced on the evening of May 24. At 8:00 p.m., British and Hessian soldiers, Royal artillerymen and Loyalist guides, totaling about five hundred men, marched from Newport to the northwest shore of Aquidneck Island. Commanded by Lieutenant Colonel John Campbell of the British Twenty-Second Regiment, the detachment was then ferried over to the Bristol County peninsula. From there, the raiding force destroyed most of the boats stashed in Kickemuit River and burned a number of houses and buildings used by Whig supporters in Warren.[72]

Legend has it that, as the British and Hessian troops marched out of Warren, a squad reportedly stopped at a house on Church Street and started cheering, after which the local schoolmaster, an Englishman named Holland, then emerged from the door and joined them. This man was reportedly the spy who provided Pigot with the intelligence for the raid.[73] This scene probably never happened.

The name of Holland as Pigot's spy, however, was accurate. Richard Holland, from Freetown, Massachusetts, had been thrown in jail as a suspected Tory in 1777. After he was freed, he made his way to British-held Newport. He earned a captaincy in the Loyal New Englanders and was stationed in Newport. From there, Holland provided intelligence to Pigot in the planning for the raid on Bristol and Warren, and he acted as a guide during the raid.[74] Apparently, an inaccurate legend later arose that he had been a schoolteacher in Warren. Significantly, a comprehensive Bristol newspaper article that described the raid on its centennial anniversary in 1878 did not mention the Holland schoolteacher story.[75]

## Spies in the Rhode Island Campaign

In late July 1778, a powerful French fleet under the command of Admiral Comte d'Estaing joined forces with American Continental, state and militia forces from New England to lay siege to British-held Newport. This was the first campaign engaged in by the new allies. The American invasion force, led by their commander, Major General John Sullivan, landed on the northern part of Aquidneck Island on August 9. When, that same day, a British fleet showed up outside Narragansett Bay, d'Estaing ordered his stronger fleet to chase after it. But just as the opposing fleets were about to engage in a classic sea battle, a fierce storm kicked up, which forced both fleets to disengage. The ensuing gale damaged the French fleet more than the British fleet. The French fleet limped back to Newport, where d'Estaing informed General Sullivan his ships required immediate repairs in Boston.

At this time, Sullivan's troops were dug in, in Middletown, opposite Pigot's defensive fortifications just outside Newport. Deciding that a frontal assault was impractical, he chose to wait and see if the French fleet would return in time to assist him. On August 28, Sullivan received word that General Henry Clinton was on his way from Long Island with a fleet of ships and four thousand troops to try to trap the American army on Aquidneck Island. Sullivan immediately ordered a night retreat north to a defensive line anchored by Butt's Hill, in Portsmouth. The next morning, General Pigot ordered British troops up the island's East and West Roads in a bid to cut off shifting American forces. But Sullivan's army fought well and held them off. The next night, Sullivan's soldiers slipped safely off the island. American army officers and soldiers alike were furious at the French for what

Ships of Comte d'Estaing's squadron at anchor. Drawing by Pierre Ozanne, circa 1778. *Library of Congress.*

they viewed as abandoning them in the middle of the siege, but they could take pride in fighting well against the enemy's regular troops and escaping from Aquidneck Island with their army intact.[76]

Spies played a role in the Rhode Island Campaign, if not a decisive one. On July 24, 1778, prior to the arrival of the French fleet, General Sullivan reversed a sentence of whipping handed out by a court-martial panel against Mansfield Allen, who had been convicted of spying. Allen, an inveterate Tory, had had an eventful prior two years. In 1777, he had fled from North Kingstown to Newport to join with Loyalist forces there. In one of the Loyalist raids on the mainland, probably in early 1778, Allen deserted the raiders and headed for New London to find work on a ship. But he was soon charged with participating in a plot with other sailors to engage in a mutiny on board a vessel and to take the vessel to Newport. Allen was confined in the guardhouse at Fort Trumbull, outside New London, to await trial. One night, he and an accomplice managed to escape amid a hail of guards' gunfire. But he was later caught and confessed.[77]

Sullivan was convinced from the evidence that Allen "was employed by the enemy repeatedly to come on the mainland as a spy, and that he enlisted men to go…into the enemy's service" at Newport. Sullivan vehemently disapproved of what he considered too light a sentence, stating that "the man who is found guilty of acting as a spy can have but one judgment by all laws of war, which is to suffer death."[78] He ordered the court-martial panel to sit again the next day at Hacker's Hall in Providence, at which, predictably, Allen's new sentence was "to be hung by the neck until he is dead."[79] There is no record of the sentence being carried out; if it had been, it likely would have been widely reported in newspapers and mentioned by diarists and letter writers.

Even after Allen's death sentence, Brigadier General James Varnum advised General Sullivan "that it is absolutely necessary to hang some person as a spy *in terrorem* to prevent intelligence from your army to the enemy. When a real spy cannot be obtained, a scoundrel, under the influence of Toryism, may be deemed a proper villain." The cold-blooded Varnum noted that the Americans had in jail Nathaniel Ketchum, "who is undoubtedly a spy," and that he might serve the purpose.[80] Ketchum, in fact, proved not to be a spy, and his life was spared.[81]

To avoid detection, American spies on Aquidneck Island frequently and wisely did not use their names in correspondence. General Sullivan received one fairly accurate and complete report of British defensive positions and troop estimates from an American spy on Aquidneck Island, probably

*The Siege of Rhode Island, taken from Mr. Brindley's House on the 25th of August, 1778.* From *Gentleman's Magazine*, London, February 1779. *Author's collection.*

around mid-July 1778. The spy refused to give his name, as by doing so, "no accident can discover me." An unidentified American officer and his two sons courageously slipped onto Aquidneck Island to meet with this spy, despite British forces being "excessive zealous and watchful."[82] The extra security imposed by the British during the Rhode Island Campaign limited the information obtained by this spy, who may have been Isaac Barker, whose espionage activities will be detailed later in this book.

Following the end of the joint American and French expedition to capture Newport, American forces assumed their usual role of defending Providence and other ports around Narragansett Bay against a possible invasion by the British forces in Newport. And the spy game continued. In September 1778, the Marquis de Lafayette, then commander of American troops on the eastern shore, attempted to set up a spy network that could infiltrate British units in Newport. Lafayette sought intelligence about the strength of the British fleet at Newport. (Admiral d'Estaing's fleet was still refitting in Boston.) On September 5, Lafayette wrote to d'Estaing, "I hope at length to find some good spies to send." Lafayette added that he had accepted the offer of an American officer who had previously crossed over to Aquidneck Island "in disguise." Lafayette also sent a fake American deserter to the island in the hopes that the soldier would be able to return to his Bristol headquarters with useful military intelligence.[83] In a follow-up letter to d'Estaing three days later, Lafayette wrote that "I am very much afraid that my spies have been hanged, for they were supposed to have given me news this morning, and I do not hear anything."[84]

Lieutenant Colonel John Laurens, a South Carolinian, one of the heroes of the Battle of Rhode Island and an aide to General Washington, indicated in a September 24 letter that the Americans had a spy on Aquidneck Island who had access to potentially significant military intelligence. He wrote, "Our spies inform us that a council of war has been held, and continued for three days."[85] At the time, Admiral John Byron and some of his large warships had arrived at Newport Harbor, raising Sullivan's concerns about a plan to invade Providence or some other coastal port.

Patriot efforts to jail suspected Tories sometimes interfered with British spy networks. At the beginning of the Rhode Island Campaign, General Pigot had one spy out, a man named Chace (a common name in Rhode Island). But Chace was identified as a suspicious person and jailed in Taunton, Massachusetts. He broke out of the Taunton jail only after the end of the campaign, in December 1778.[86]

## Ann Bates: British Spy Extraordinaire

One of the few known female spies on either side in the Revolutionary War, Ann Bates spied for the British during the Rhode Island Campaign. She provided her British handlers with valuable intelligence, despite never setting foot in the state. However, she did not, as some historians claim, play a crucial role in the British triumph.

Born around 1748, Bates worked as a schoolteacher in Philadelphia. Because her husband, Joseph Bates, was a soldier and gun repairman in the British army, she learned about weaponry and the importance of military information, such as the enemy's cannon, soldier and supply totals. At some point during the British occupation of Philadelphia, Ann Bates met with John Craig (sometimes Craiggie or Cregge), a civilian active in Clinton's espionage network. Craig judged her, accurately, as it turned out, to be intelligent and resourceful—just the right type to thrive as a spy. Bates performed a few secret tasks for Craig.

The Bates family's world changed dramatically when General Clinton, the new commander in chief of British forces in North America, decided to evacuate Philadelphia, in response to news of the alliance between France and America and Admiral d'Estaing's possibly imminent arrival in the

Delaware River. After her husband joined Clinton's army, which marched out of Philadelphia on June 18, 1778, bound for New York City, Ann followed. When, on about June 26, she arrived in the city serving as British headquarters, she asked to see Craig. Instead, she was taken to meet with one of Clinton's spy handlers, Major Duncan Drummond. Drummond and Craig persuaded Bates to spy for the British army. Drummond subsequently wrote: "A woman whom Craig has trusted often came to town last night. She is well acquainted with many of the R.A. [Royal Army]….It is proposed to send her out under the idea of selling little matters" in Washington's camp, and there "she will converse with Chambers and will return whenever she may have learnt anything that deserves to be known."[87] Craig later received a nice finder's fee from the British secret service for bringing Bates to Drummond's attention.[88]

After a mere single day of training, on June 29, Ann departed New York City on her first mission. Using the cover name Mrs. Barnes, Bates disguised herself as a peddler. She was given five guineas for expenses to buy items for a peddler's pack—thread, needles, combs, knives and some medicines. On July 2, she arrived at Washington's camp at White Plains, New York. As Mrs. Barnes, she freely traveled among the American soldiers and camp followers. Bates had been instructed by Drummond to find a disloyal soldier, named Chambers, and to glean any useful intelligence from him. However, she could not find him. Bates then resourcefully changed her mission to find out what useful intelligence she could on her own. She listened in on conversations and counted artillery pieces. After finally selling most all of her merchandise, she made her way back to Drummond in New York City.

Bates began to spy on Washington's army at a time when it was sending Continental regiments eastward to augment Sullivan's army in Rhode Island. On July 29, 1778, Major Drummond dispatched Bates back to White Plains. Still disguised as Mrs. Barnes, the peddler, she evaded or passed through multiple military checkpoints and finally arrived at Washington's camp. She was again unable to locate Chambers, her contact. (She learned later that he had been killed in a battle in the Mohawk Valley.) Bates therefore spent the next three or four days wandering about the American camp, counting "119 pieces of cannon" and estimating the number of soldiers at twenty-three thousand. She spotted ten wagons rolling into camp "with wounded" in them. She also described the locations of the American brigades. She even boldly entered the residence temporarily being used as Washington's headquarters and spotted the commanding general, but did not learn any useful information there.[89] "During her stay amongst them," Drummond

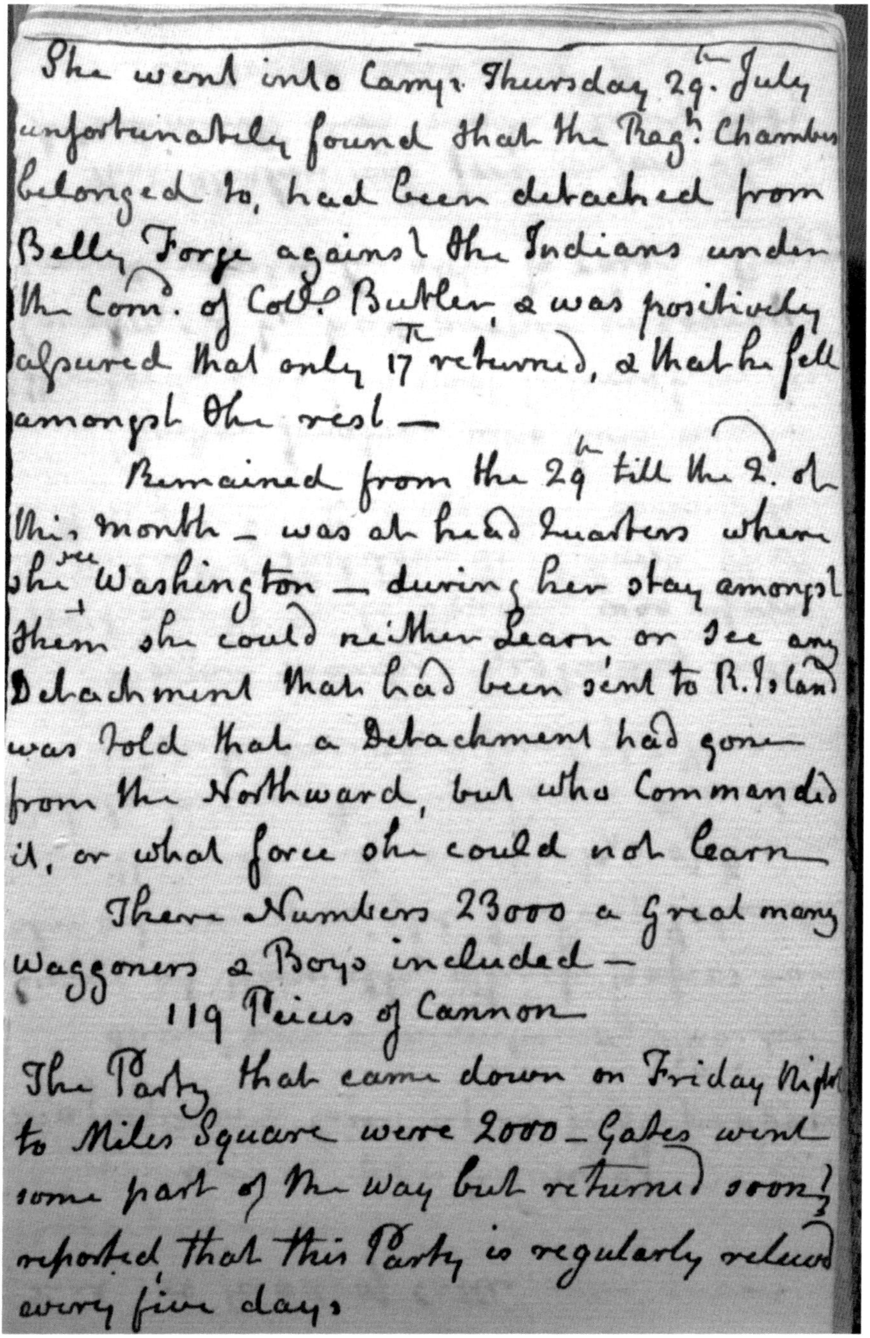

She went into Camp. Thursday 29th July
unfortunately found that the Regt. Chambers
belonged to, had been detached from
Valley Forge against the Indians under
the Comd. of Coll. Butler, & was positively
assured that only 17 returned, & that he fell
amongst the rest—
Remained from the 29th till the 2d. of
this month—was at head Quarters where
she see Washington—during her stay amongst
them she could neither Learn or See any
Detachment that had been sent to R. Island
was told that a Detachment had gone
from the Northward, but who Commanded
it, or what force she could not Learn—
There Numbers 23000 a Great many
Waggoners & Boys included—
119 Peices of Cannon
The Party that came down on Friday Night
to Miles Square were 2000—Gates went
some part of the way but returned soon;
reported that this Party is regularly relieved
every five days

Copy of a page from a British memorandum book of reports from spies and others, probably prepared by Duncan Drummond. The "she" and "the woman" referred to is Ann Bates. *Library of Congress.*

wrote after Bates's return to New York City on August 6, "she could neither learn nor see any detachment that had been sent to Rhode Island."[90]

Just two days later, Bates was sent back to White Plains for a third time, arriving on August 12. At Washington's headquarters, she overheard an officer who she thought was a general inform one of Washington's aides-de-camp (perhaps Alexander Hamilton) that six hundred boats were being prepared for an invasion of Long Island by 5,000 troops (this attempt was never made). She also learned that about 3,000 Continentals and 2,000 militiamen had left camp for Rhode Island. Bates observed that with the departure of another detachment of 3,800 "picked men" to Dobbs Ferry, the American camp "was not near so numerous as when she was first there, nor their parades half so full." She estimated the strength of Washington's army had fallen to 16,000 or 17,000 troops. She counted fifty-one pieces of artillery on Saturday and saw nine more cannon arrive in camp the next day.[91]

Bates took pride in her role, writing in a petition for a pension in 1785 that "my timely information was the blessed means of saving the Rhode Island garrison with all the troops and stores who must otherwise have fallen a prey to their enemies." Duncan Drummond was asked to review Bates's petition. He observed, "She asserts nothing but what is strictly true" and that "her information...was by far superior to every other intelligence."[92] Paul R. Misencik, who recently wrote a detailed history of Ann Bates's espionage activities, called her Britain's "most effective" spy, in large part based on her supposed decisive role in the Rhode Island Campaign.[93]

Bates's role in the Rhode Island Campaign has been exaggerated. Most importantly, the timing is off. Early in the morning of July 22, 1778, Continental brigades commanded by James Varnum of Rhode Island and John Glover of Massachusetts, totaling 2,500 soldiers, set out on their 160-mile trek to Rhode Island. Later that morning, Washington appointed Major General Marquis de Lafayette to command the detachment, forcing the young French nobleman to gallop off to catch it.[94] Lafayette's Continentals reached Tiverton, Rhode Island, the staging area for the invasion of Aquidneck Island, on August 8. Accordingly, when Bates reported to Drummond on August 6 that no American troops had yet left for Rhode Island, she was incorrect. In addition, on August 19, after her next trip to the White Plains camp, Bates told Drummond of the movements of the two Continental brigades. She added that 2,000 militiamen accompanied this detachment, but this too was inaccurate.

When Bates returned to Clinton's headquarters on August 19 and belatedly warned of American troop movements to Rhode Island, it is said that this information led Clinton to reinforce the Newport garrison, which helped to defeat the combined French and American forces outside Newport.[95] However, this could not be accurate, as Clinton never sent any reinforcements to Newport in August because the French fleet had arrived outside Narragansett Bay on July 29. Back on July 9, concerned that Newport would be exposed to an attack by the French fleet when it arrived, Clinton had prudently sent some 1,850 troops, under Major General Richard Prescott, by boat through Long Island Sound to reinforce the Newport garrison.[96] However, this was weeks prior to Lafayette's Continentals departing White Plains for Rhode Island on July 22.

Still, Ann Bates was a remarkable woman and a valuable spy. Her ability to handle the physically grueling trips between her posts without resting long and getting past the many Continental army checkpoints was impressive. The intelligence she provided was timely, since Clinton was then planning his own attack on Sullivan's army before it left Aquidneck Island. Ultimately, Clinton's force, collected at Long Island, arrived one day too late to trap Sullivan.

Bates's efforts proved that women could be valuable spies. They were often able to overhear secret information because they were considered unable to understand the complexity of military affairs. Disguised as a mere peddler, she was able to penetrate even Washington's headquarters. Bates was paid for each of the three trips she made to Washington's camp—twenty dollars, thirty-one dollars and thirty dollars.[97]

# 5

# Return to the Status Quo and the British Depart

## October 1778 to October 1779

### Metcalf Bowler: Rhode Island's Benedict Arnold

Prior to the start of hostilities with Great Britain, Metcalf Bowler was one of the wealthiest and most prominent Patriots in Rhode Island. An Englishman by birth, he settled in Newport as a young man, later becoming rich as a privateer owner and merchant. It was said that he owned one of the only two coaches, pulled by "an elegant span of horses," in the colony.[98] Bowler was so respected that he was elected speaker of the House of Deputies twice a year from 1767 to 1776, and he served as a justice of the Rhode Island Superior Court from 1768 to 1776, becoming its chief in his last year of service.[99]

Bowler had impeccable credentials as a Patriot. One of the colony's two delegates to the Stamp Act Congress, he also served as a member of the Sons of Liberty and Newport's Committee of Correspondence.[100] To celebrate the anniversary of the repeal of the Stamp Act, the March 18, 1767 edition of the *Newport Mercury* reported: "In the evening, Hon. Metcalf Bowler, at his house at the corner of Clarke and Mary Streets, gave an elegant entertainment to the true friends of liberty." On April 25, 1775, after learning of the Battles of Lexington and Concord, as speaker of the House of Deputies, Bowler wrote to the Massachusetts Provincial Congress: "Notwithstanding an exception of a very few individuals, you may be assured

Anne Fairchild Bowler, wife of Metcalf Bowler. Painting by John Singleton Copley, circa 1763. *National Gallery of Art.*

that the colony is firm and determined, and that a greater unanimity scarce ever prevailed in the Lower House than was found in the great questions before them."[101]

Bowler kept a fine house in Newport, but during the British occupation, it was used as a hospital for the British Forty-Third Regiment.[102] Accordingly, he and his family resided at his stately mansion and farm in Portsmouth. Indeed, one of the wood-paneled rooms from this house would be later removed and installed in the Metropolitan Museum of Art in New York City. During a lull in the Rhode Island Campaign, a Massachusetts chaplain took a stroll "to view a garden near our quarters belonging to one Mr. Bowler—the finest by far I ever saw," despite the damage it had suffered from wartime neglect.[103]

Bowler's personal firmness and determination deserted him four days after the British occupied Newport in December 1776. Bowler sent General Clinton a letter, proposing "to submit myself to His Majesty's clemency…"[104] He was probably motivated in part by a desire to protect his house, library and garden, as well as his farm. In this first correspondence with Clinton, Bowler requested that a guard be sent to his house to protect him from the "insults of the Hessians." Bowler explained that "the Hessian troops are quartered on the island and hav[e] committed many outrages and depredations, on many of the inhabitants, by entering their houses, and plundering their effects, and even putting them in fear of their lives."[105]

Clinton immediately met with Bowler, who gave the general a stack of official Rhode Island state papers to review.[106] In return, Clinton gave Bowler some money. Bowler's bargain did little for his property. As a result of a British regiment camping next to the house for most of eighteen months, his farm lay "in waste," all of his fence posts were removed for firewood, his sole surviving cow was stolen and butchered by troops, his last four horses were taken for use by British army officers and his library was "plundered of sixty odd volumes."[107]

Clinton did not forget Bowler. The British commander in chief made a short visit to Newport in early September 1778, after his fleet arrived from Long Island. During his stay, Clinton met with Bowler and asked him to serve as a spy. In order to protect the former Patriot's identity, Clinton offered Bowler the ability to send correspondence directly to him at his headquarters in New York City, by using Captain Henry Savage, an aide to General Pigot and deputy quartermaster general for the troops in Newport, as a messenger. Fully cognizant of the danger of committing to such work, Bowler accepted the assignment on September 15 on the conditions that Clinton mention his name to no one and let no one else read his letters other than Clinton.

Bowler advised Clinton that while he had a source for intelligence on the mainland (probably in Providence), the man would "be afraid to correspond frequently with me here, owing to the difficulty of conveyance and apprehension of being detected."[108] Instead, he proposed to his high-ranking spy handler in New York City that he be permitted to move from British-occupied territory to Providence. Bowler was confident that from there he could have his sealed messages, signed by his pen name Rusticus, conveyed to British officers in Newport, who could then have the messages delivered by ship to Clinton. Bowler also thought that such a move would facilitate his appointment to the Rhode Island Council of War, his election to the Rhode Island General Assembly and possibly his selection as one of the state's two delegates to the Continental Congress. In return, Bowler asked to be paid for his services. (He fatuously described the money as reimbursement of election expenses.)[109]

It is not clear what motivated Bowler to think of moving to the mainland. He needed to provide for his family, which he was unable to do in British-occupied Newport. Certainly, Bowler was limited in the services he could perform for his spymaster if he remained on Aquidneck Island. Regardless, in October 1778, Clinton agreed to Bowler's bold proposal. The Rhode Island General Assembly also had to approve the move, which it did in February 1779.[110]

Bowler's prediction that he would be welcomed back in Whig circles in Providence proved overly optimistic. He perhaps did not realize that by remaining on Aquidneck Island during the British occupation, he would arouse suspicion. He compounded concerns by leaving behind his adult daughter, Bathsheba, to watch over his property in Portsmouth. The spy informed Clinton, "My daughter being left behind has caused great suspicion here and I am rather watched with a jealous eye."[111]

Bowler nevertheless began his work for Clinton. He also had second thoughts about leaving his daughter on Aquidneck Island, perhaps under pressure from his Whig friends. On April 9, 1779, Horatio Gates, the new American commander in chief in the Rhode Island theater, gave Bowler permission to send a boat to Newport to pick up Bathsheba and the rest of his family.[112]

Suspicion of Bowler lingered. Responding to a false rumor that Bowler's luggage contained counterfeit money, Patriot authorities searched all of his possessions.[113] The former Newport merchant never was allowed back into the inner councils of state government. In 1779, he was given only minor committee assignments.[114] Bowler told Clinton that he rejected important positions in the Rhode Island government, claiming that he could obtain more information as a private citizen. It seems unlikely he was ever offered these positions. While Bowler claimed he was on good terms with General Gates, which enabled him to gain useful intelligence occasionally, he could have gained far more as a member of the Rhode Island Council of War. Clinton must have been disappointed. Bowler's correspondence contained much information obtainable by any alert civilian.

Bowler set up a small dry goods store in Providence, but he had difficulty buying merchandise to sell. He was eventually reduced to selling whatever items his Newport spy contacts could provide him with. Pathetically, the man who was once one of the richest in the colony even requested stock from Clinton, such as "a few pieces of black and tailored ribbons," "a few green shoe bindings," "one or two dozen more black handkerchiefs" and similar small items. He further asked that "a good case coat" be thrown in for him to wear in the upcoming winter months, which he claimed would facilitate his ability "to pick up intelligence."[115]

It is not clear who performed the dangerous task of serving as intermediary between Bowler in Providence and Captain Savage in Newport. It could have been British spies or Loyalists staying at a safe house in Providence. In any event, they did their job well and were never caught. On one occasion, Bowler's own mother carried information from her son to Savage.[116]

Bowler reported false rumors that an American army under General Sullivan was preparing to invade Canada and that the French fleet was expected at any time in June 1779 to cooperate in another move against Newport. Bowler also reported the occasions when new American commander Major General Horatio Gates feared a British raid, and he gave Clinton the names and locations of American regiments stationed around Aquidneck Island. He further described the faltering American economy—the rapid depreciation of American currency and increasing prices for food and supplies.[117]

One historian claimed that none of Bowler's military intelligence sent to Clinton "was of much importance"; and another argued that "Bowler was not a good agent."[118] While those assessments are for the most part accurate, some of the intelligence conveyed by Bowler, including information of troop stations and troop numbers, was useful. In addition, in a letter dated July 13, 1779, Bowler provided Clinton with the valuable information that Glover's Brigade of Continentals had just marched from Providence to New London to protect against an expected British raid there, and that Providence was only defended by Colonel Henry Jackson's "small regiment" of Continentals. Bowler thought that because local farmers were

Major General Horatio Gates. *Library of Congress.*

working hard on their farms, it would be difficult for the Americans to raise more than one thousand militiamen quickly. Accordingly, he advised Clinton that the British should "strike while the iron is hot" and raid Providence.[119] Providence was indeed vulnerable at this time. Bowler wrote that he had visited Boston and had found it equally poorly defended.[120]

By now, however, Clinton was no longer interested in raiding either city. Indeed, unbeknownst to Bowler, Washington had withdrawn Glover's Brigade from Providence after hearing that Clinton had removed 1,500 of his troops from Newport on June 25.[121] Nonetheless, Bowler's shocking recommendations indicate that he either deeply desired a British victory in the war or simply harbored a deep resentment of Rhode Island leaders who had shut him out of the highest government jobs.

Bowler may have played a key role in Clinton's decision to evacuate Newport. Between June and October 1779, he repeatedly reported that Gates expected the French fleet under Admiral d'Estaing to reappear in Narragansett Bay at any time to threaten Newport. He described Gates giving orders to repair the flatboats, for thirty men at all times to produce gun cartridges, for wagon drivers and the artillery train to be ready to move on a moment's notice, for soldiers to cut fascines used for fortifications and for planks for artillery platforms to be cut at saw mills.[122] Out of fear of d'Estaing's arrival, on October 7, 1779, Clinton issued orders to evacuate Newport.

It turned out that Gates did not know where d'Estaing would end up any more than Clinton. The French admiral wound up sailing to Savannah, Georgia, where his forces suffered a crushing defeat.

Bowler worried constantly about being exposed as a spy. Early on, he pleaded with his handler, "I must entreat your Excellency would keep the whole that passes between us in your own breast, for should it ever come to the Provincial's knowledge of my correspondence, nothing short of my life would pay the forfeit."[123] Clinton kept his word about maintaining Bowler's identity a secret, and his role as spy and traitor remained undiscovered for the remainder of Bowler's life. His treason was not discovered until the 1920s.[124]

Bowler was certainly an enemy spy and a traitor to the American cause. However, there are degrees of being a traitor. He was not as bad a traitor as Benedict Arnold, who received large sums of money and took command of British armies in the field to oppose the Americans. In contrast, Bowler did not become rich from serving as Clinton's spy, and he never took up arms against the Whigs. He was more like Dr. Benjamin Church, who received pay from British spymasters in exchange for providing them with secret intelligence while he was serving as a high-ranking Continental army officer.

## Isaac Barker, Seth Chapin and Spying in Middletown

The most successful American spy in the Rhode Island theater was Isaac Barker, a twenty-six-year-old farmer whose farm and house in Middletown were about three and one-half miles east of Newport.[125] Belonging to the sixth generation of Barkers living in the area now known as Paradise Valley, Barker became a farmer and carpenter before he married a local woman,

Sarah Peckham, in 1775. He began providing General Sullivan with intelligence about British military operations on Aquidneck Island sometime after the Battle of Rhode Island in August 1778. He was most active in the summer and fall of 1779, when he worked for General Gates. From April 1779 until the British departure from Newport on October 25, 1779, at least thirty-eight messages were sent to Gates and General Ezekiel Cornell of Scituate, containing intelligence obtained by Barker.[126] Barker worked with his brother, Samuel Barker.

Barker was aided by his handler, Lieutenant Seth Chapin of Colonel Henry Sherburne's Additional Regiment of Continentals. Chapin, from Mendon, Massachusetts, had served in Tyler's Regiment of Massachusetts militia from December 8, 1776, through January 21, 1777, during the "alarm" created by the British invasion of Newport. He then served in Colonel Benjamin Haw's Regiment of Massachusetts militia in the Rhode Island Campaign, before transferring to Sherburne's Additional Regiment of Continentals in August 1778.[127]

Beginning in September 1778, the twenty-four-year-old Chapin was stationed in Little Compton in command of a whaleboat operated by eight men who guarded the coastline and kept an eye on Aquidneck Island. Chapin demonstrated his courage in December 1778 when he and his whaleboat crew captured a British brig whose captain had sailed into the Sakonnet River due to adverse winds.[128]

Chapin's crew included a relative of Barker's, Hezekiah Barker, who resided in Little Compton and served as the boat's pilot. William Taggart Jr., who had assisted his father's spying activities during Spencer's Expedition, was also a crew member up to March 1779.[129] Chapin and his boatmen probably resided on the family farm of Patriot colonel Perez Richmond, near the Little Compton shoreline on the south side of the present Blockhouse Lane.[130] From there, or even better, after taking a short walk farther south to a small peninsula jutting into the Sakonnet River called Church Point, Chapin would have had a clear view of messages from Barker on the opposite shore.

Barker and Chapin agreed on an arrangement by which Barker would alert Chapin when he had information to convey. According to Barker's 1833 application for a pension for his service in the Revolutionary War, Barker communicated with Chapin by "telegraphic signals" made with a "stake and a crutch and a stone wall." Barker had agreed on a code with Chapin, so that details about British and Tory ships—their number, whether they were armed and where they were headed—could be sent to Chapin across the channel in Little Compton by viewing the positions of the stake and crutch on the stone wall. Barker explained that there were as many as seventeen different positions, each of which had a different meaning, which allowed him to send up to fifty or sixty different signals. The stone wall ran along the top of the ridge of Great Rock, a granite formation that was the highest geographical point on Aquidneck Island and just a short walk from Barker's house. The distance from the eastern bank of the Sakonnet River to the Great Rock inland from the western bank was approximately one mile, so Chapin had to use field glasses (then called a "spy glass"), which were not common at the time.

A crude map drawn by Barker and submitted as part of his pension application features two "bar ways" (or wood-post gateways that could allow a cart in a field) on the south and north sides of the ridge. Barker set his signals at and between these two points. Neither of these gates exists today, but according to authors James L. Yarnell and Natalie N. Nicholson, the "south bar way" was at a break in a ridge a half mile north of Second Beach, and the "north bar way" was three-tenths of a mile further up the ridge.[131]

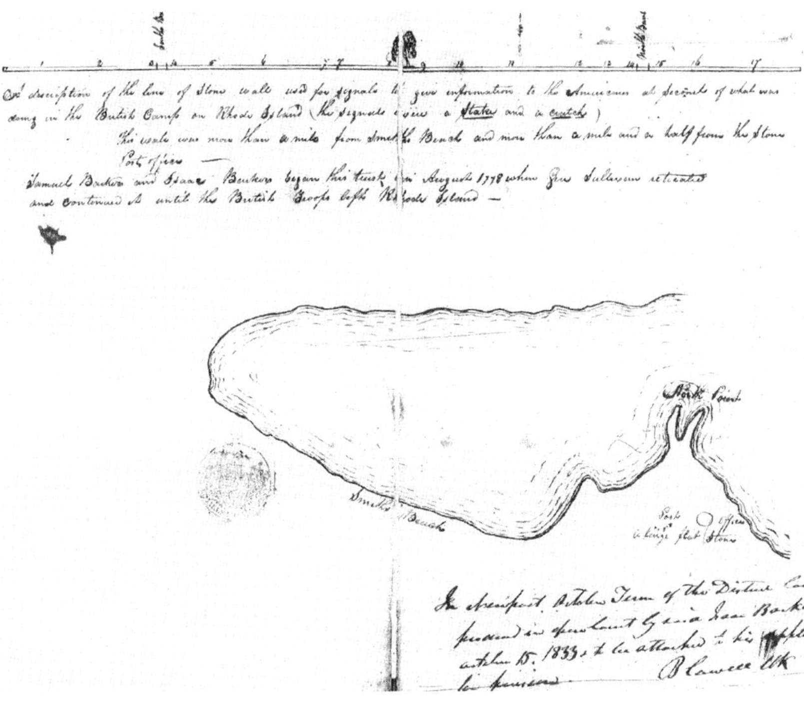


Map in Isaac Barker's Revolutionary War pension application, 1833. The upper portion shows the "telegraphic" signals. *National Archives.*

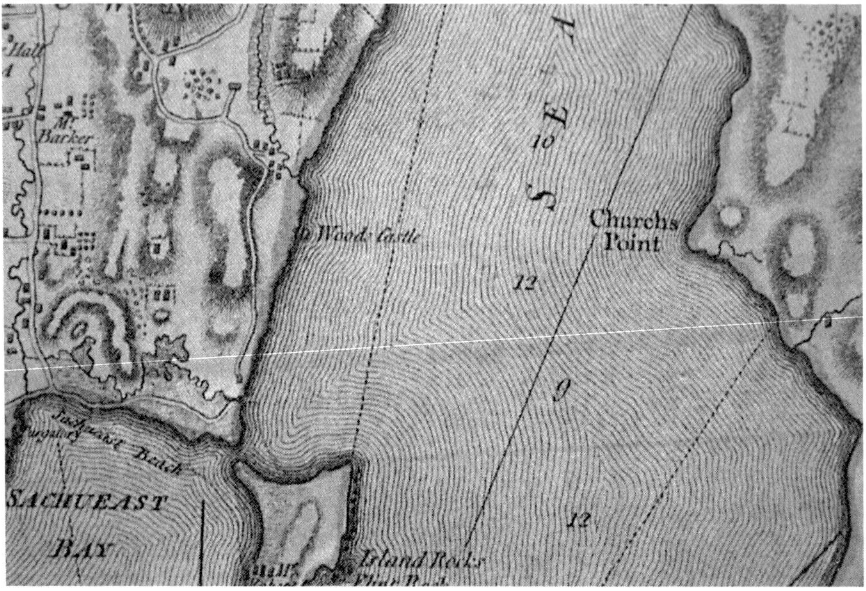


Detail of map showing the Barker house, a short distance from the Sakonnet River and Wood's Castle. From *A Topographical Chart of the Bay of Narragansett* by Charles Blaskowitz, London, 1777. *Library of Congress.*

Sometimes, the "telegraphic message" indicated that a personal meeting was requested. At these times, Barker recalled, "a boat came over in the night, at the time indicated." Chapin's crew would be met by Isaac or Samuel Barker, who would convey the intelligence, after which Chapin's crew would return to Little Compton.

Barker had to be extremely careful because a British regiment frequently camped near his home, during which time its colonel resided in Barker's house, which was located at the current 485 Paradise Avenue, in the eastern part of Middletown. The British officer's presence was also a benefit, as he frequently and unwittingly conveyed intelligence to Barker.

In April 1779, General Ezekiel Cornell explained to General Horatio Gates, shortly after the latter assumed command in the Rhode Island theater, the activities of Chapin and Barker (without identifying Barker by name):

> *Lieutenant Chapin of Col. Sherburne's Regiment has been stationed at Little Compton since last September with a party of observation, during which time General Sullivan looked upon the intelligence through that channel the best he received. In which time he* [Chapin] *has fixed upon certain signals to be thrown out in the day time from the house where*

> *his correspondent dwells that can be discerned by him on this side. One* [signal] *announces some movement of the enemy. Another when the guard and sentries are in such a situation that he* [Chapin] *can with probability of safety go on* [Aquidneck] *Island. Another when he cannot, which was the case yesterday, together with many more* [signals].[132]

In his correspondence with Gates, Cornell would use a code to identify Chapin and his secret agent (Barker), rather than their actual names.

In that same month of April, the British began to strongly suspect that messages were being sent from the area around Barker's house and "stationed a regiment in that neighborhood; and quartered some men in every farm-house, to detect the persons concerned." It was then, Barker stated many years later, that he and Chapin "had to invent another plan in addition to the stake signal, which was as follows: A flat stone on the north part of Sachuest Point, near the shore, was agreed upon, under which all printed or written communications were deposited by each party, to be exchanged."[133] According to authors Yarnell and Nicholson, the location of this "stone Post Office" is what has since the eighteenth century been called Wood's Castle or Castle Rock (today called Lion's Rock). Because of towering cliffs, this

View of Castle Rock, or Wood's Castle, with the Sakonnet River and Little Compton shoreline to the east in the distance. *James L. Yarnall.*

The gap behind Great Rock, with Amy Barker, a descendant of Isaac Barker, at the bar way looking east, about 1910. This is the "north bar way" noted on Isaac Barker's handwritten map. *Private Collection.*

rocky islet was difficult to spot from the Middletown coast, but could be seen easily from Perez Richmond's farm across the Sakonnet River. This made it a perfect secret depository.[134]

On seeing either the north or south bar ways left open—the signal that a written message would be delivered that night—Chapin and his crew would wait until dark and then row over to Castle Rock to retrieve it. Back in Little Compton, Lieutenant Chapin would turn the message over to the American commander on the Tiverton side, General Cornell. William Wilkinson, Cornell's secretary, would read Chapin's abominable handwriting to his superior, who would then forward the intelligence report to the American commander in the Rhode Island theater, first Sullivan and subsequently Gates.

Later, to reduce the risk of being caught, a window in Peleg Peckham's barn was left open to signal that intelligence reports were waiting under the flat stone. The Barkers also obtained official permits from British authorities that allowed them to fish in the Sakonnet River. None of the island's inhabitants were allowed on the shoreline except to fish. When they did not have their own fishing permits, the Barker brothers even boldly borrowed them from their neighbors in order to provide cover.[135]

Isaac Barker wrote in his pension application many years later, "Had he been discovered, he would have lost his life, but fortunately he escaped detection." Benjamin Cowell, who helped Barker prepare his pension application in 1833, recounted one incident in which the spy was almost caught:

> *Isaac said that he came very near being caught one night, returning from the "Post Office." He was overtaken by two light horsemen* [British dragoons], *and a "pass" or "countersign" was demanded. It so happened he had neither. He managed, however, to get them to return with him to his house instead of making him a prisoner. On their arrival, he made up a story to the Colonel, who ordered him* [Barker] *to be released. But there was one time he had great difficulty to retain his self-possession. The Colonel was one day at dinner when he called Barker to come into his room. "Barker," said he, "there is a traitor or spy among us—there is no mistake—not a single thing transpires on this island but the rebels know all about it almost as soon as we ourselves. This traitor must be found out. Let me but see him, and the rascal shall soon go into eternity." Barker told us it required all his strength of nerve to conceal his feelings; he knew the "rascal" was then in the presence of the Colonel; but with strong language he coincided with the British Colonel, "yes," said he, "the traitor ought to be hung," and he promised to help search him out. After this, he was more of a tory than ever.*[136]

Barker's messages contained useful intelligence. He frequently described preparations by outgoing British and Tory fleets, as well as the soldiers they carried and their rumored destinations. From Barker, American officers learned details of George Leonard's fleet of Tory ships prior to many of his raids emanating from Newport. In one instance, General Cornell used information supplied by Barker to warn a small contingent of Massachusetts militia on the Elizabeth Islands that Leonard's fleet was headed his way, allowing them to remove sheep to keep them from the Tory raiders.[137] On another occasion, Barker provided intelligence of hundreds of Tory troops preparing to embark on a raid of Connecticut towns in July 1779. He kept track of the identities and locations of British, Hessian and Tory regiments, as well as enemy fortifications, on Aquidneck Island. In early October, Gates forwarded one of Cornell's letters containing intelligence from Barker to Samuel Adams in Boston, adding, "It comes from a person who is never deceived in the information he procures from Rhode Island."[138]

On January 13, 1779, General Cornell, writing from Tiverton, alerted General Sullivan to important intelligence conveyed by Barker. This letter indicates Barker's tenacity. Cornell wrote:

> *Some of Chapin's men were on Rhode Island last night and the person who they correspond with informed them that the enemy has got a number of boats hauled down near Black Point, and that they were collecting forces by volunteers, as was supposed to make a descent upon some part of the mainland. The correspondent* [i.e., Barker] *had not seen the boats himself, and was not able to ascertain their number, but was determined to see them and the party is to meet again on Friday night, when he thought he* [Barker] *should be able to give a more particular account of the movements of the enemy.*[139]

Sullivan, on another occasion, informed the president of the Massachusetts Council that British preparations to invade the mainland were "confirmed by an officer sent on" Aquidneck Island "in disguise."[140] He likely meant Lieutenant Chapin. The reference to his being "in disguise" is significant. If Chapin did not wear his uniform when he met with Barker, he risked hanging as a spy if he were caught.

Chapin wisely never conveyed Barker's name and identity to any American officer, not even with Gates or Cornell. Tory civilian sympathizers and British spies frequently overheard discussions among American officers.

Barker's and Chapin's spy activities were never uncovered by the British. According to Isaac Barker, he and his brother "were rewarded a small degree by General Gates afterwards," but Isaac turned his award over to his brother and co-spy, Samuel.[141]

## The Spy Game Continues

In October 1778, General Sullivan sent Sergeant Henry Brown into Newport as a spy. Brown came out of Newport safely and conveyed, according to an aide to General Washington, "very useful intelligence" regarding British operations in New York.[142]

In December 1778, Brigadier General John Stark of New Hampshire, then second in command in the Rhode Island theater of war, reported to Sullivan, "I am informed by the spy Mr. Cahoon that a ship arrived in

Newport which he took to be a ship of the line. She had lost her main mast, mizzen mast and fore top gallant mast and bowsprint." This arrangement must not have lasted long, as there are only a few references to this spy.[143]

Brigadier General John Stark. *Author's Collection.*

Mr. Cahoon was likely one of eight adult Cahoon men listed as residing in Newport in the 1774 census.[144] The spy was likely either Charles Cahoon or John Cahoon Jr., who were both sent to the Newport prison ship as suspected Whig sympathizers during the panic in Newport that followed with the discovery of Spencer's Expedition in October 1777.[145]

The American command engaged in counterspy activities. In late November 1778, after hearing reports that the British had sent six spies to the mainland, sixty soldiers from the Second Rhode Island Regiment of Continentals were sent to Providence to "take up" strangers.[146] On January 15, 1779, in his general orders, General Sullivan complained that a British spy, after being captured aboard a provision vessel that had arrived in Tiverton, managed to escape back to Aquidneck Island. "As there is reason to believe that the enemy has a number of spies on the main, the officers will be particularly attentive to prevent their escaping," Sullivan ordered.[147] According to clandestine traitor Metcalf Bowler, after General Horatio Gates assumed command from Sullivan, he warned that "the first person he catches conveying intelligence, he will directly hang."[148] He also placed a sentry on the "Great Bridge" leading to Providence with orders to interrogate all persons crossing to the town and to bring to him any person who could not provide a decent explanation of why he or she was going to Providence.

Despite American counterespionage activities, following the Battle of Rhode Island, the British were able to start to rebuild their spy network, taking advantage of Tories residing in the countryside and towns. For example, on November 7, 1778, British commanders in Newport received intelligence of a "secret" American attempt to send vessels from Providence to capture the British frigate *Sphynx*, then stationed in Narragansett Bay. In response to this information, the vessel's commander beefed up the ship's defenses.[149]

Sometimes, information from spies convinced the British to cancel raids. In March 1779, the British navy came close to sending several frigates up Narragansett Bay to burn shipping at Providence. Before committing to the raid, Admiral James Gambier of the Royal Navy waited for reports from spies sent to the mainland by General Prescott in Newport. One spy observed that while Providence was lightly defended, there was "no shipping of consequence in Providence River." This report was forwarded to Gambier and Clinton, along with another note: "General Prescott further says a person is now employed to find out the exact state of Warren, Providence, and places adjacent. I expect him to return on Saturday night."[150] Gambier heard enough from the first spy's report and called off the raid, deciding that merely destroying a few vessels at Providence's wharves was not worth the risk and effort.[151]

In the meantime, Sullivan's spy network had caught wind of Gambier's plans. The New Hampshire general received "repeated intelligence" from Aquidneck Island that the enemy was preparing to make a descent on the mainland. This intelligence may have been from the spy Isaac Barker. Sullivan had the plan confirmed by an American officer spy sent on Aquidneck Island,[152] who may have been Barker's handler, Lieutenant Seth Chapin.

In October 1778, the Americans caught the notorious Tory from Newport who had been part of Walter Chaloner's spy ring, William Crossing. While he was convicted of marauding, plundering and seizing Whig leaders in their houses and sentenced to hang, he was also charged as a spy. In a letter to General Prescott trying to justify the harsh sentence, General Sullivan compared Crossing's treatment to "the late Captain [Nathan] Hale who was executed at New York by orders of General Howe."[153] However, Crossing was more raider than spy. In any event, before his sentence could be executed, he escaped from a Providence jail and fled to the safety of Newport.[154]

In part influenced by the reports of Metcalf Bowler that the Comte d'Estaing's fleet was bound for Newport in the fall of 1779, General Clinton ordered his army to evacuate Aquidneck Island. General John Stark, keeping a close eye on the fleet of transports intended to carry troops to New York City, finally wrote General Gates on October 25 that the British were "gone, gone, gone!"[155]

When Stark's troops entered Newport, they found that while the British forces had departed, many Tories had not. General Prescott, concerned that his fleet could not carry all of the Loyalists and their belongings and worried that they would become a burden to the Crown in New York City, had advised most of them to stay put, and many had listened.[156] This meant that embedded in Newport were potential spies to operate in Clinton's secret service network.

## Other Sources of Intelligence

Sending out spies was not the most common intelligence-gathering approach, even if it was the most dangerous. Commanders on both sides had a variety of sources for gathering information: deserters from enemy regiments, freed prisoners, civilian escapees and their own officers who went on board "flag ships" to enemy ports for the purpose of exchanging prisoners or delivering correspondence to the enemy's commanding general.

Military deserters were an important source of intelligence. Even General Washington gave advice to General John Sullivan on how to gain useful information from them. After receiving from Sullivan what he perceived to be an inflated estimate of enemy troops on Aquidneck Island, Washington advised him, "The most certain way of calculating the enemy's strength is first to ascertain the number of regiments, and then endeavor to find out the number of men in them by examining deserters and others."[157] All of the American commanders of the Rhode Island theater forwarded estimates of British, Hessian and Tory troops to General Washington, mostly based on information from deserters.[158] One British deserter made it easy for American officers by carrying with him an official British orderly book that contained the identities and sizes of the British regiments in General Charles Grey's expedition force that had just raided nearby Bedford and was about to land at Martha's Vineyard in September 1779.[159] As another example, British major Frederick Mackenzie reported that an American deserter had arrived two days before with the significant news that the "rebel" frigate *Warren*, then stationed near Providence, was planning "to come down the first fair wind, in order to proceed to sea."[160]

In May 1779, General Horatio Gates acquired accurate information from two Hessian deserters from the von Ditfurth Regiment, both surgeon's mates, who estimated the size of each of the British, Hessian and Tory regiments on Aquidneck Island. The deserters further suggested that the best approach for an American ship to sail up to Providence and avoid the British blockade was to sail past the lighthouse at Beaver Tail at the southern tip of Conanicut Island and head up the West Channel.[161] In September 1779, a British deserter from the Thirty-Eighth Regiment accurately reported that General Prescott was "in great apprehension of a visit from either the French or Spanish fleet."[162]

In one sad case, on October 14, 1779, a British soldier attempted to desert from northern Aquidneck Island to Tiverton, but he was pursued by a party of British guards. An American boat attempted to rescue the deserter, but he was mortally wounded before the Americans could reach him. While wounded, the deserter passed on intelligence that the British commanders intended to evacuate Newport and that all the heavy cannon and baggage had already been loaded onto transport ships. The deserter, who had desperately sought to leave the British army and remain in the state and start a new life, died a short time later.[163]

Military deserters sometimes gave inaccurate information as well. For example, on July 22, 1778, General Sullivan interpreted a British move to reinforce Conanicut Island as a precursor to a British invasion of Providence, as a result of a British deserter who claimed that the British "design is to burn Providence, which is to be done next Thursday night."[164] Based on this false information, Sullivan issued an alarm leading to hundreds of militiamen mustering and rushing to Providence for no reason.

Between Aquidneck Island and the mainland, there was a sporadic flow of civilians, who often had useful intelligence to convey. Captain Hare, a Tory, was stuck in Providence when the British first occupied Newport. He was able to deliver a letter to Newport containing accurate information of Providence's defenses and an estimate of the American troops in and around Providence.[165]

A few days after issuing the alarm based on the faulty intelligence from the British deserter in July 1778, Sullivan received more accurate information from a civilian escapee from Aquidneck Island, an African American who had been a servant for British commander General Pigot. He reported that "the enemy are busily employed in fortifying both on Conanicut and near Newport" and that "there were Hessians and Waldeckers in the last reinforcement from New York."[166]

African American civilians were a good source of information, perhaps because whites underestimated their ability to understand and convey military intelligence. This was a mistake. Major Frederick Mackenzie, in his diary entry for June 30, 1777, recorded information that two African American civilians who escaped from the mainland to Newport divulged to the British command.

> *Two Negroes came over from Narragansett this day. They say the country people are in the greatest confusion, and that many of those on the coast are removing farther into the interior, as they expect to be visited by the King's troops. That the paper money is so much depreciated, that hardly anything is to be got for it. That the currency of one province will not pass in another. That provisions are scarce and dear, and very little corn to be had. And that they find it so difficult to raise men for the Continental Army that they enlist Negroes, for whom their owners receive a bounty of 180 dollars, and half their pay, and the Negro gets the other half, and a promise of freedom at the end of three years.*[167]

In one of the outstanding special operations of the war (which was highlighted in a recent book by the author, titled *Kidnapping the Enemy: The*

*The Capture of General Prescott.* Prescott stands in his nightshirt, ready to be taken across the bay following his capture. The hats worn by the American soldiers are like the ones worn in the 1830s, when the engraving by an unknown artist was made. *Catherine Williams,* Biography of Revolutionary Heroes *(1839).*

*Special Operations to Capture Generals Charles Lee & Richard Prescott*), during the night of July 10, 1777, Lieutenant Colonel William Barton and a hand-picked detachment of forty-seven other Rhode Islanders departed from Warwick Neck and crossed Narragansett Bay in whaleboats, sneaking past British navy ships along the way. After landing on Aquidneck Island, Barton carefully led his men along a path to the farmhouse in which Major General Richard Prescott, the commander of British troops on the island, spent his nights. The raiders forced open its doors and seized the sleepy British general in his bed. They then hurried to their boats and slipped back across the bay to Warwick Neck, their quarry in hand, avoiding a flurry of British artillery and rocket fire.[168]

The key intelligence for the raid was provided by two civilians. A white civilian, Paul Coffin, escaped from Aquidneck Island and, on June 20, informed Barton in Tiverton that General Prescott was spending nights at the Overing farmhouse in Portsmouth about five miles north of Newport. This information led Barton to arrive at the idea of organizing a small party of men to abduct the British general.

Barton also gained valuable information about the Overing house and its guards from Quako Honeyman, a former African American slave who had been pressed into service as Prescott's servant and who had recently escaped from Aquidneck Island. His "great and essential service" later led the General Assembly to release him from bondage.[169] Major Mackenzie, an aide to Prescott, wrote that Barton and his men "received the most perfect intelligence" and that they "must have been thoroughly well informed of the position of the guards and sentries, as they could not possibly have come a nearer or better way to [Prescott's] house."[170]

Prisoners who were exchanged or escaped sometimes acquired useful information that they passed along. As a result of interviewing prisoners held by the Americans and returned to the British in February 1777, General Percy learned that the Americans had only about 5,250 troops in the entire Rhode Island theater, including only 150 at Warwick Neck and 1,000 at Providence.[171] General Howe in New York used this information to conclude that Percy had no "reason to apprehend an attack from [General] Arnold" and to request that Percy send him troops from Newport for use in his New Jersey campaign.[172]

Sometimes, officers who captained "flags of truce"—ships carrying prisoners for exchange or correspondence for enemy leaders and flying a white flag—gained useful information from talkative opponents and by noticing their surroundings. While Lieutenant John Trevett took advantage of a flag of truce to sneak from tavern to tavern in Newport gathering intelligence (as described in chapter two), it was the British who benefitted most from them.

In early February 1777, while attempting to organize the first expedition against Newport, General Arnold complained to Washington that "I am fully convinced that by means of these flags the enemy will be acquainted with our most secret movements."[173] Arnold was right to be suspicious. The British officer leading the flag, Philip d'Auvergne of the HMS *Chatham*, when he arrived in Providence, talked to an aide who had been with Washington's army (perhaps John Trumbull Jr. of Connecticut) and who told him that he had been trying to raise troops in Rhode Island for weeks and had only recruited three men.[174] D'Auvergne gave British commander Percy accurate information regarding American troop strength.[175] General Howe also relied on this information to conclude that the Americans would not attack Newport and to order Percy to send some of his troops back to him.[176] Only a week later, Captain Richard Smith of the Royal Navy, who led a flag of truce into Bristol on February 15, 1777, reported to General Percy about Bristol's defenses.[177]

Captain Henry Barry, sent on board a flag of truce vessel from Newport to meet with Rhode Island officials to discuss the treatment of the recently abducted General Prescott, was not permitted to sail to Providence. Instead, he met Rhode Island officials on board the Continental navy's *Providence* frigate off Pawtuxet (now Cranston). Barry later provided General Percy with the following description of that warship: "She is really a fine frigate carrying twenty-six guns, but badly manned and ill-armed, she not having more than a hundred hands on board, mostly landsmen, and the guns being both too short and heavy."[178]

If an officer on a flag of truce was caught engaging in improper activities, the backlash could be harsh. Early in October 1777, Admiral Sir Peter Parker sent the sloop *Friendship* to Providence, under the command of Lieutenant Charles E. Nugent and carrying women and children wanting to leave Newport. By October 13, the sloop and Nugent had not returned, and Parker wrote to Governor Cooke to complain. In fact, Nugent had been caught making sketches and taking soundings in the Providence River and was rightfully detained by the Americans. After Governor Cooke replied on October 14 with the reasons for detaining Nugent, Admiral Parker became concerned that Rhode Island authorities might jail Nugent or worse. Governor Cooke generously allowed the young lieutenant to return to Newport on November 15, shortly after the secret Spencer's Expedition ended.[179]

Americans also acquired intelligence from escaped prisoners. In September 1779, two French sailors escaped from a military hospital in Newport, after recovering from a bout of scurvy that raged on a British frigate they were forced to work on. The Frenchmen reported that the British generally believed that Admiral d'Estaing "is on the coast" and would "attack them" in Newport.[180]

Americans further gained intelligence from prisoners taken from captured vessels. In one instance, the Tory sloop *George*, one of George Leonard's vessels operating out of Newport, was captured off North Kingstown during a raid. On board the sloop was the wife of an imprisoned British officer who conveyed to her American examiners a detailed and accurate report of the positions of British ships in Newport Harbor.[181]

The Americans had the benefit of lookouts along the southern Rhode Island coast. State and county soldiers manned observation posts at Tower Hill in South Kingstown to report on British vessels arriving and departing from Newport. They also manned other posts as far west as Watch Hill, in order to spot enemy fleets in Long Island Sound. The Americans had advanced warning of the initial British invasion of Newport in December 1776, in part due to coastal lookouts.

On two occasions, American military authorities clamped down on civilians, deserters and spies traveling to British-occupied territory: during Spencer's Expedition in October 1777 and the Rhode Island Campaign in August 1778. Each time, the British commanders, frustrated by the lack of information they received, resorted to the brazen tactic of kidnapping civilians behind American lines. On August 2, 1778, before the French fleet had entered Narragansett Bay but after the British had abandoned Conanicut Island, a party of men from the British Twenty-Second Regiment landed on Conanicut Island and forcibly brought off two inhabitants. The information they gained was startling in its detail and fairly accurate, indicating how information about military plans swept through Rhode Island communities:

> *The account these people give is that a very formidable attack will be made upon us very soon; Sullivan, with 15,000 men being in our neighborhood; and* [Lafayette] *on board the French fleet with a brigade of Continental troops, which they took in off Delaware. It is expected that by the 5th instant 20,000 men will be assembled for the expedition. They talk of making four different attacks, viz, one from Conanicut or Prudence Island, one on the east side from Fogland under cover of the French frigates; and the principal one on the north end of the island from Howland's Ferry....D'Estaing, who commands the French fleet, is pressing them to commence their operations as soon as possible, but the rebels are not yet in readiness.*[182]

When Sullivan's army later landed on Aquidneck Island and marched to the British defensive lines outside Newport, the British were again frustrated by the lack of military deserters and Tory civilians escaping to British lines with information. Major Mackenzie wrote in his diary, "We are at present almost wholly without intelligence of the enemy's real strength, situation or intentions. All the inhabitants of the adjacent country are our enemies, and the difficulty of getting in [to British lines] is too great to induce any person to come in with intelligence. I am inclined to believe we do not pay liberally for it."[183]

On August 21, 1778, the British again resorted to sending a party in a whaleboat to Conanicut Island and taking off a civilian, who accurately informed the British that the New England militia's terms had expired or were about to expire, that they were tired of the expedition and disillusioned now that the French fleet—which they had depended on in the first instance—had departed for Boston, that d'Estaing's fleet was shattered by the storm and that d'Estaing was unlikely to return to Newport. At about 1:30

a.m. on August 23, Colonel Edmund Fanning led 150 men of his Loyalist King's American Regiment quietly out of their redoubt. Creeping up to an American picket post, Fanning's troops attacked, killing one man with a bayonet and successfully taking two prisoners. The next night, a British party landed at North Kingstown and captured a farmer and his slave.

Finally, on August 24, the first American deserter escaped to British lines, a sergeant in Colonel Henley's Regiment. The deserter accurately informed the British that the American militia was displeased with Sullivan, that there were only seven battalions of Continental troops on the island and that the rest of the army was composed of militiamen who were tired of the expedition and ready to depart for their homes. But the deserter and kidnapped persons did not know what the British wanted most to discover: whether or not Sullivan planned to attack or retreat, and if he planned to attack, where that would occur.

Early on the morning of August 26, two men from Colonel Fanning's Loyalist regiment captured an American sentry, but he knew nothing of Sullivan's plans. The next night, two soldiers from the same regiment crept out of British lines to capture a pair of American sentries, who, in putting up a struggle, made a "great deal of noise," leaving the attackers "under the necessity of killing them." Then, on August 26, an American deserter entered British lines and provided accurate information detailing American plans to retreat to the northern part of the island and stating that the American troops were "in hourly expectation of seeing the British fleet, which they hear amounts to eighteen men-of-war and transports with 3,000 troops."[184] The deserter was describing Clinton's expeditionary force from Long Island. Back in the American camp, Thomas Quigley of Webb's Regiment of Continentals was convicted of attempting to desert to the enemy and summarily hanged.[185]

British commanders still complained of being "extremely deficient in the most certain means of procuring accurate and authentic information."[186] Four parties were sent out to capture more men who might have additional information, only one of which succeeded.[187] Mackenzie's lament, coupled with desperate British efforts to capture American civilians and soldiers in order to obtain information, demonstrates the importance the British placed on accurate military intelligence.

# 6

# The French Occupy Newport

## July 1780 to August 1781

### The French Arrive, and the Adventures of Thomas Hazard

From July 1780 to August 1781, a French fleet and army occupied Newport, Rhode Island. The port town served as the primary base of French operations in the United States during the war, and the French soldiers and sailors would play a key role in the stunning French-American victory at Yorktown in Virginia, which effectively won the war for the allies. But that was not known in July 1780. In July 1780, General Clinton felt that if the combined forces of the British navy and army could attack Newport after the French arrived but before they established their defenses, they could gain a crushing victory that might take France out of the war.

On April 27, 1780, a ship carrying Major General Marquis de Lafayette arrived in Boston. The French aristocrat conveyed stunning news to John Hancock and a few other select Whig leaders: when he sailed from France, an expeditionary force of seven ships of the line and four frigates under Admiral Chevalier de Ternay, along with thirty-six transport vessels carrying about six thousand French soldiers commanded by Lieutenant General Comte de Rochambeau and their supplies, was preparing to leave the port of Brest, France, for North America, with the destination of Newport, Rhode Island.

It was crucial that news of the impending arrival of the French fleet be kept secret. If British commanders learned of it, the Royal Navy could try to intercept Ternay's fleet, or combined British army and navy forces could attack Newport before the French had time to establish their defensive works. This goal of maintaining secrecy was, however, not easy to accomplish in freewheeling New England.

A member of Lafayette's entourage, Lieutenant Colonel Louis-Dominique Éthis de Corny, had orders to make the necessary commissary arrangements for the arrival of Ternay and Rochambeau. Among Corny's first tasks was to establish a hospital in Providence, for the expected hundreds of sailors and soldiers who would become ill during the long Atlantic crossing. Corny wanted to use what is now University Hall at Brown University. But fearful of the disease the sailors and soldiers would bring with them, the Providence town meeting on June 15 resolved "to adopt legal and proper measures to prevent the establishment in this town of a hospital for receiving the sick on board the fleet of His Most Christian Majesty daily expected to arrive in this State from Europe."[188] The General Assembly, meeting in South Kingstown, supported the Providence town meeting, but Corny and the Rhode Island Council of War quashed the effort on June 25.[189] Still, Tories or General Clinton's spies could have easily learned of this ugly dispute.

New England newspapers did not publish news of the expected arrival of the French fleet at Newport, save for one. In the June 1, 1780 edition of the *Massachusetts Spy*, which was based in Worcester, the following item appeared: "We are informed that intelligence was brought to the governors of Rhode Island and Connecticut a few days past, that a French fleet may be hourly expected at Newport, New London, or some of the neighboring ports."

Newport was the logical destination, as it had a deep-water port for handling large ships. While it was common for newspapers to copy interesting news items appearing in other newspapers, this ill-advised item was not re-published in any other newspaper, and was not picked up by Clinton's spies.

On June 12, Clinton's spy network learned of the expected arrival of the French fleet at

General Sir Henry Clinton. London, 1780. *Anne S. K. Brown Military Collection, John Hay Library.*

Newport from a spectacular source: Benedict Arnold, then Major General of the Continental army.[190] This was after Arnold had decided to provide the British army with intelligence but a few months before he fled the American army for the protection of New York City and exposed that he had become a traitor. Arnold's information was succinct and quite accurate: "Six French ships of the line, several frigates, and a number of transports with six thousand troops are expected at Rhode Island in two or three weeks."[191] Clinton later asserted that this intelligence was Arnold's most important service and the main justification for the large cash payments made to him.[192] Arnold had learned the information after Lafayette's May 10 arrival at Washington's headquarters.[193] Arnold advised Clinton that the Royal Navy should intercept the French fleet before it landed at Newport.[194]

Clinton would have to cooperate with Admiral Marriott Arbuthnot, commander of the Royal Navy in North America, but he would find that a challenge to say the least. "General Arnold's intimation that the French [fleet] intended to touch at Rhode Island having suggested to me an idea of attacking their troops immediately upon their landing there," recalled Clinton after the war. "I prepared a select corps with every other necessary apparatus for a sudden embarkation, and requested the Admiral to order transports to be held in constant readiness for the reception of 6,000 men on the shortest notice."[195]

On June 29, 1780, two Rhode Island Tories, John Nichols and Joseph Goddard, arrived in New York City after departing Newport several days earlier. They reported to British general James Robertson that Newporters had been expecting the arrival of the French fleet "for a fortnight."[196]

On July 7, two British ships brought intelligence to Admiral Arbuthnot that their spotters had picked up the French squadron off the coast of Virginia heading northward. Clinton quickly came up with two plans for destroying or capturing French forces in Newport. The first was for the British ships of the line to blockade the exits of the Narragansett (Middle) Channel in order to prevent the French warships from interfering with Clinton's land invasion. Clinton then would "go into the Sakonnet Passage with 5,000 men and a sufficient number of frigates to cover my landing."[197] This first alternative was intended to attack enemy forces "before they could have time to throw up works for their defense." The alternative plan, in case the French had time to erect formidable defenses, was for Arbuthnot's fleet to sail up the Narragansett Channel, to anchor in between Conanicut Island and Aquidneck Island and to land Clinton's troops near Newport Harbor.[198]

Meanwhile, Washington called on the services of his successful Culper spy ring, based in Long Island, for intelligence of Clinton's movements. "As we may every moment expect the arrival of the French fleet a revival of the correspondence with the Culpers will be of very great intelligence," wrote the commander in chief to Major Benjamin Tallmadge, the talented Continental officer who handled the spy ring.[199] Tallmadge first contacted Captain Caleb Brewster, who took his sailboat across Long Island Sound from Connecticut to Setauket, Long Island. Finding his and Tallmadge's boyhood friend and spy, Abraham Woodhull, sick in bed, Brewster then sought out Austin Roe, a tavern keeper in East Setauket. Roe rode almost nonstop to New York City and met with the ring's key spy, Robert Townshend, a dry goods storeowner and part owner of a coffeehouse frequented by sometimes loose-lipped British officers.

Townshend soon learned of Clinton's large ground force gathering on the north side of Long Island and passed on a letter containing the explosive intelligence to Roe. The same day, Roe rode the fifty-five miles back to Setauket and delivered the letter to a still-ailing Woodhull. (Woodhull's spying activities were highlighted in the recent television series *TURN* and were the focus of the recent best-selling book *George Washington's Secret Six: The Spy Ring That Saved the American Revolution*.) Woodhull forwarded the letter to Brewster, along with (as historian Alexander Rose put it), "the most urgent note he ever penned."[200] Woodhull advised Brewster, "The enclosed [from Townshend] requires your immediate departure this day by all means, let not an hour pass for this day must not be lost. You have news of the greatest consequence perhaps that ever happened to your country."[201] Brewster rushed back across Long Island Sound to the Connecticut shore and, bypassing Tallmadge to speed delivery of the message, dispatched a rider to Washington's headquarters to the west. At Preakness, New Jersey, Alexander Hamilton, one of the commander in chief's young aides, received the message the afternoon of July 21. The time of Washington's initial request to Tallmadge to Hamilton's receipt of the intelligence was a mere ten days.

Hamilton read Townshend's intelligence that the British were aware of the expected arrival of the French fleet at Newport; that nine powerful British warships had departed from New York and had "sailed for Rhode Island"; and that "8,000 troops are this day embarking at Whitestone," Long Island, with a design to attack the French at Newport.[202] Even though Washington was away, Hamilton immediately penned a letter to Lafayette, who had left Washington's headquarters on July 19 for Newport in order to help coordinate military affairs

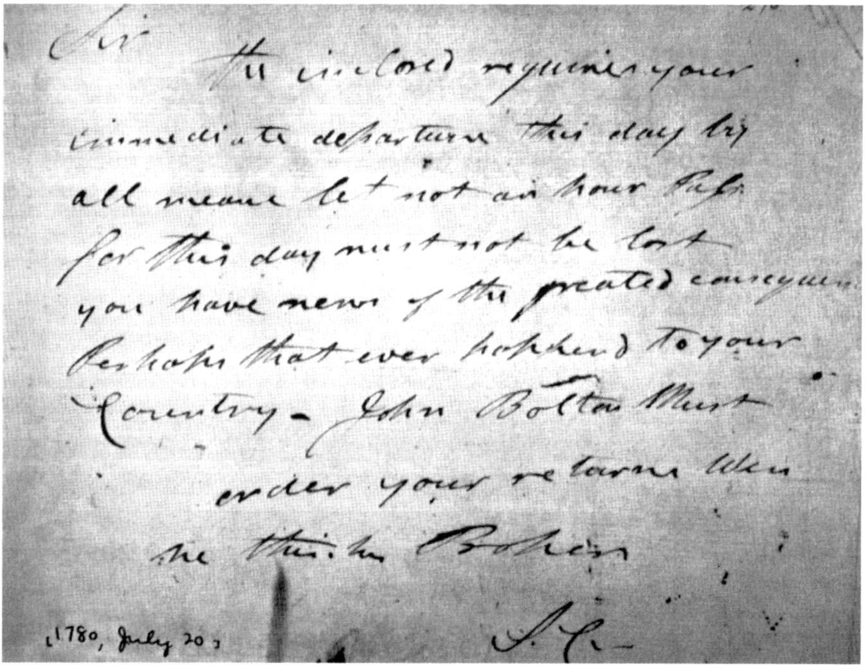

Sir
The inclosed requires your
immediate departure this day by
all means let not an hour pass
for this day must not be lost
you have news of the greatest consequen
perhaps that ever happened to your
Country. John Bolton Must
order your return when
he thinks [illegible]
S. C—
1780, July 20

Image of letter penned by the Culper spy ring's Abraham Woodhull, who warned against an invasion of Newport and called it the most urgent letter he ever sent. *Library of Congress.*

between Rochambeau and Washington. The young colonel stated that he had "just received advice from New York through different channels that the enemy are making an embarkation with which they menace the French fleet and army. Fifty transports are said to have gone up the Sound to take in troops and proceed directly to Rhode Island."[203] A bit after 4:00 p.m., he sent an express rider eastward to catch up with Lafayette.

At the time, the Continental army was camped west of the Hudson River. When Washington returned to his Preakness, New Jersey headquarters, he used the Culper spy ring's intelligence to prepare for a diversionary attack outside New York City at the key point of Kingsbridge, New York, in the hope of causing Clinton to call off his planned expedition against Newport.[204]

On July 18, Clinton received shocking news: the French fleet had arrived outside Narragansett Bay on July 10.[205] To Clinton's dismay, not only had Arbuthnot's ships lost track of the opposing fleet; they had not become aware of Ternay's arrival in Newport for a full week.

Clinton still wanted to attack Newport, implementing either his plan to land troops in the Sakonnet River or in the Narragansett Channel. At

this time, a fleet under Rear Admiral Thomas Graves, having arrived at New York City from England, was unloading seven hundred sick sailors and replacing them with available hands. The combined naval ships of Arbuthnot and Graves would be superior to Ternay's fleet in Newport.

Still, the French took time getting their defenses in order. Starting on July 13, the healthy troops began to disembark. By July 15, they were all ashore, hard at work repairing the forts abandoned by the British nine months earlier and building new ones at the south end of Aquidneck Island. On July 16 and 17, the approximately 1,500 sailors and 800 soldiers and marines sick with scurvy and other illnesses contracted during the seventy-day Atlantic crossing were disembarked. Those ill soldiers not taken to Newport's churches were transported by small boats

*Top*: The Comte de Rochambeau. From a painting by J.D. Court. *National Archives.*

*Left*: The landing of the French troops in Newport on July 11, 1780. *Library of Congress.*

to hospitals Corny had established at Providence, Bristol and Papasquash Point.[206] The next important matter was getting ashore the artillery, which was crucial for fending off any land or sea attack. On July 21, ten days after their arrival, all of the field artillery was on land and placed in position.[207] "In twelve days' time," wrote Rochambeau in his memoirs, the defense of Newport was "rendered respectable."[208]

The British commander in chief desperately sought intelligence of the number of French troops, the number of American reinforcements, their cannon and the condition and locations of the defenses they were erecting. For this mission, he called upon Captain Henry Savage, who had handled the spy Metcalf Bowler from Newport in 1778 and 1779.

After a crucial delay getting his troop transports ready, by July 22, Arbuthnot had his North American squadron cruising outside of the entrances to Narragansett Bay. On the same day, Clinton sent on board the twenty-eight-gun *Iris* Captain Savage and seven or eight "trusty inhabitants of that country [Rhode Island], to obtain such intelligence as I could act from."[209] These men were Rhode Island Tories who had departed with the British army's evacuation of Newport in October 1779. Savage and his intrepid volunteers sailed aboard the *Iris* to a point near the entrances to Narragansett Bay. The plan was to set the volunteers in a whaleboat, probably at night, and have them land near Newport. But the *Iris*'s commander, Captain James Hawkes, refused to cooperate, purportedly because he did not wish to lose one of his valued whaleboats. A frustrated Clinton, after learning of the matter, added in a letter to Sir William Eden, "And my aide-de-camp [Captain Savage], of course, would not send them to certain sacrifice without being assured by Captain Hawkes he would at least attempt to bring them off."[210] Clinton later recalled, "Captain Savage rejoined me in Huntington Bay on the 30th, without having been able to put on shore any of the people he carried with him, or to procure any further intelligence respecting the enemy than we had before."[211]

On July 26, Clinton received a letter from Arbuthnot stating that the admiral had personally viewed, from the deck of his own flagship, enemy troops erecting fortifications on Brenton Neck and "a very large encampment on the beach on the south end of [Aquidneck] Island fronting the sea," which would oppose Clinton's landings.[212] Unsatisfied with this report, Clinton expressed annoyance that "no certain intelligence had even yet been procured of their operations."[213]

Meanwhile, in the afternoon of July 25, the two allied commanders at Newport—Major General William Heath of Massachusetts, the head of

American forces in the Rhode Island theater, and General Rochambeau—received the first intelligence of Clinton's attack plans. But, contrary to the conclusions of some historians covering the famous Culper spy ring, the first word did not arrive from the express rider dispatched by Alexander Hamilton. This rider never caught up with Lafayette prior to the French general arriving in Newport on July 24.[214]

The first word received by General Heath of Clinton's plans came in the sloop *Gates*, whose captain boldly sailed it from Stonington, Connecticut, evading the British blockade of Narragansett Bay and arriving at the Newport wharves about 3:00 p.m. on July 24. The sloop carried Colonel Samuel B. Webb, a colonel of a Continental army regiment named after him, who was then on parole as a former prisoner. After he had been captured on a transport vessel in Long Island Sound during a mission and brought to Newport in December 1778, Webb had been generously and quickly paroled, and allowed to reside at his home in Wethersfield, Connecticut. On learning of the arrival of the French fleet from Major Tallmadge, Webb, along with four of his Connecticut friends, had decided to sail to Newport and visit their Newport friends and the newly arrived French officers, almost as a lark.[215] However, it was a risky adventure, since their boat could have been intercepted by a British frigate.

After leaving the central Connecticut coast on July 18 and leisurely making their way eastward, Webb and his friends arrived in Stonington, Connecticut, on July 23 and heard the stunning news of Clinton's imminent attack on Newport. When they arrived in Newport the next day, they brought with them a written statement from Clark Pratt, who had left Long Island on July 23, probably by whaleboat. On Long Island, Pratt had met a man who had departed New York City on July 21. This man had informed Pratt that Admiral Graves had arrived from England with his ships of the line, that he had landed his sick sailors, recruited one thousand volunteers to replace them and had proclaimed that Newport was their destination. The same man informed Pratt that British troops had embarked onto ships carrying them eastward, that they numbered ten thousand and that they were on transports poised to make the perilous passage through Hell Gate in the East River and onward to Newport. The author of the report stated that both Pratt and the man who had been at New York City "are both known in Stonington to be of veracity."[216] Webb's actions, delivering valuable intelligence against the interests of the Crown, violated the terms of his parole, but he felt that the news was too important to leave to others.

Heath then immediately penned the following to Rhode Island's governor William Greene:

> *Intelligence this moment received by the way of Long Island that Sir Henry Clinton intends to make an attempt on Rhode Island with a large body of troops, it is said ten thousand men. His Excellency Count de Rochambeau requests that he may be immediately reinforced with two thousand militia. I request that you would order fifteen hundred of that number properly officered, armed and accoutered to rendezvous without the least delay at Tiverton. General Rochambeau says that in six or seven days, he shall be*

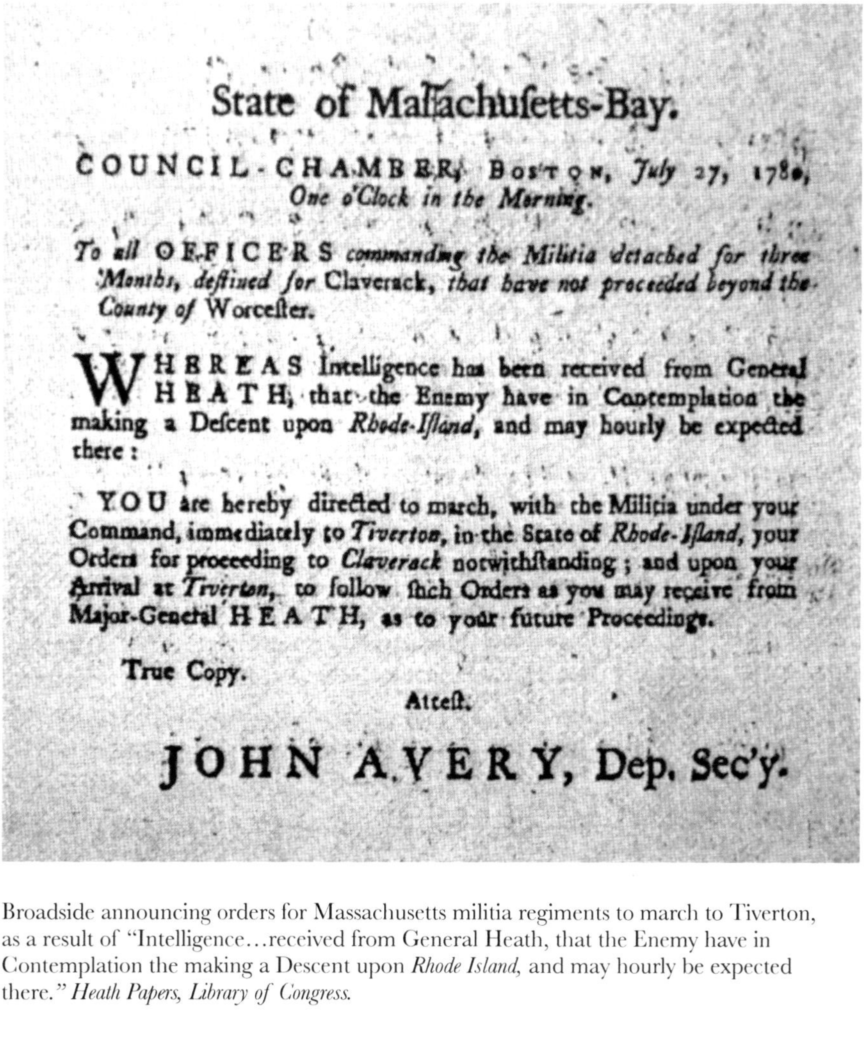

State of Maſſachuſetts-Bay.

COUNCIL-CHAMBER, BOSTON, *July* 27, 1780,
*One o'Clock in the Morning.*

*To all* OFFICERS *commanding the Militia detached for three Months, deſtined for* Claverack, *that have not proceeded beyond the County of* Worceſter.

WHEREAS Intelligence has been received from General HEATH, that the Enemy have in Contemplation the making a Deſcent upon *Rhode-Iſland*, and may hourly be expected there:

YOU are hereby directed to march, with the Militia under your Command, immediately to *Tiverton*, in the State of *Rhode-Iſland*, your Orders for proceeding to *Claverack* notwithſtanding; and upon your Arrival at *Tiverton*, to follow ſuch Orders as you may receive from Major-General HEATH, as to your future Proceedings.

True Copy.

Atteſt.

JOHN AVERY, Dep. Sec'y.

Broadside announcing orders for Massachusetts militia regiments to march to Tiverton, as a result of "Intelligence…received from General Heath, that the Enemy have in Contemplation the making a Descent upon *Rhode Island*, and may hourly be expected there." *Heath Papers, Library of Congress.*

> *perfectly secure without them, and they may return home at that time.... The account says the enemy has embarked.*[217]

Heath wrote a similar letter to Brigadier General George Godfrey—who commanded Massachusetts militia hailing mainly from the neighboring counties of Bristol, Plymouth and Barnstable—requesting an additional eight hundred soldiers.[218]

The Culper spy ring's message was not the second warning to arrive in Newport either. That honor went to Colonel Henry Babcock from Westerly, Rhode Island, who had in 1776 commanded a Rhode Island regiment, but had been sacked by the state's general assembly. Babcock, it seems, had met the same man, C. Clark Pratt, who had recently arrived from Long Island at Stonington. After repeating the same intelligence, Babcock added, "The person who brought me the above intelligence from Long Island is a young man of undoubted veracity and son to a member of the Assembly of New York State, who fled from Long Island and lived a year without his family in my house at Stonington, and he may be relied upon. He says the person who informed him is a man of character." Babcock sent his children's tutor, a Mr. Whitman, to deliver the message on July 24. Despite the weighty matter addressed in his letter, Babcock made a trivial request of Heath to allow Whitman to board Ternay's flagship, "as Mr. Whitman was never on board a ship of the line."[219] Babcock sent a second message the next day, after receiving a confirming report from another man who had just departed from Long Island and arrived at Stonington, as well as word from another "gentleman" who added that "the British officers flatter themselves of entirely captivating both the Fleet and Army of His Most Christian Majesty."[220]

An express rider carrying Hamilton's dispatches from Preakness, New Jersey, finally arrived at Lafayette's quarters in Newport just before midnight on July 25. While he was writing a letter to Governor James Bowdoin of Massachusetts, requesting more militia, General Heath added the following postscript: "P.S. 12 o'clock at night. By a letter this moment received from headquarters, the intention of the enemy against this place is confirmed."[221]

In the next few days, other reports of Clinton's preparations to invade Newport arrived at Heath's headquarters. One came from Major Benjamin Tallmadge, who sent his message separately, in case Hamilton's messenger had been waylaid.[222] Hamilton, as a result of "receiving advices through different channels from New York" of the British embarkation, sent a second dispatch to Newport on July 21, this one addressed to General Rochambeau.[223] Major General Robert Howe, based in the Highlands of

New York State, received accurate intelligence of Clinton's intentions from a "variety of agents," and, on July 23, dispatched to Heath an express, which arrived in Newport probably on July 27 or 28. Brigadier General Samuel Parsons, based in Danbury, Connecticut, wrote Lafayette on July 24 of British naval and army movements, which led him to "believe the enemy designs to attack the ships and troops at Rhode Island."[224] On July 28, Heath wrote to Governor Greene, "The intelligence received here of the motions and probable intentions of Sir Henry Clinton was from Colonel Hamilton at headquarters, Major General Howe, General Parsons, Major Tallmadge, some gentlemen at Long Island, and other sources from thence."[225]

After the dispatch from Colonel Hamilton arrived, Heath took the threat even more seriously and issued requests for all of the militia of Rhode Island and more militia from Massachusetts to gather at Tiverton or Bristol. In addition, lookout posts with fire-burning coal lamps used as signals were established from Tower Hill in South Kingstown to Watch Hill in Westerly. (Washington soon established a chain of posts for "relays of dragoons every fifteen miles" from Watch Hill to New London and to his headquarters to the west.)[226]

Meanwhile, by the morning of July 28, more than seventy transport vessels carrying Clinton and his troops were anchored in Huntington Bay off Long Island. The soldiers, broiling in the summer sun, waited impatiently for orders to proceed with the attack on Newport.[227] Before ordering the attack to proceed, Clinton wanted to hear the latest intelligence and whether or not Admiral Arbuthnot would be a willing participant.

On July 30, at Huntington Bay, Captain Savage conveyed to Clinton the intelligence he had obtained as an eyewitness. Captain Charles Hudson of the *Richmond* had sailed up to the entrance of the Narragansett Channel, where Savage, despite the hazy weather, had plainly seen that "three small encampments were formed upon Brenton Neck and a large one on the heights over the town of Newport [probably Miantonomi Hill]. On the Island of Conanicut a large work was being erected, upon the high ground by the Dumplings Point that forms an entrance of the harbor. Possession also appeared to be taken of a barrack not far distant, and some tents pitched nearby." Savage added information obtained by Arbuthnot that "the French had obtained a large rebel force in addition to the 5,000 men they had brought with them, and had raised works and mounted a great many pieces of cannon."[228]

Who was the source of Arbuthnot's intelligence of the "large rebel force"? It appears it was brought by Thomas Hazard, a staunch Tory from North Kingstown and Newport. Known as "Virginia Tom," probably due to

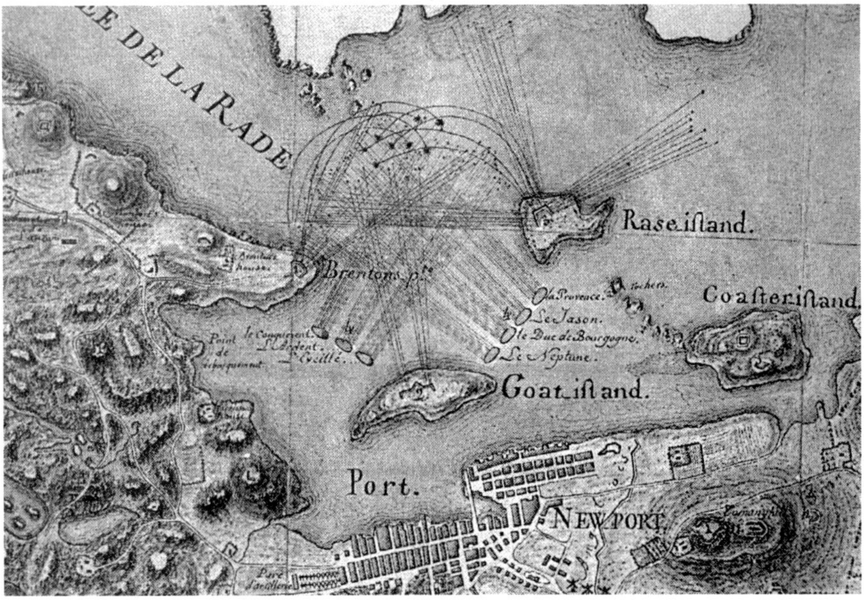


Detail of a French map showing the positions of the French ships of the line in a crescent shape protecting Newport Harbor and showing the firing lines of the ships and land artillery from Brenton's Neck and Rose Island. *Library of Congress.*

his first marriage to a woman from Virginia, and in order to differentiate himself from a score of other Thomas Hazards in southern Rhode Island, Hazard had left his North Kingstown farm and become a moderately successful Newport privateer captain and merchant.[229] Following the British occupation of Newport in December 1776, Hazard took an active role in local military affairs. In his post-war claim for reimbursement of wartime losses, writing in the third person, he explained that "he obtained a small vessel by order of General Prescott, manned with sixteen Refugees [fellow Loyalists] to bring off some men left on an island near Conanicut Island [probably Dutch Island], and then they proceeded to the main, went on shore, and brought off a flock of sheep. Was pursued by two privateers but maintained a running fight and got safe into [Newport] with the sheep for the use of the garrison." Afterward, on May 8, 1779, Hazard joined forces with a band of Tory raiders from Newport led by George Leonard. "We went by my advice to Point Judith and brought off eleven hundred sheep (one hundred of which was my own property). Also brought off sixty head of cattle all for the use of said [Newport] garrison." Several days later, on May 20, Hazard and another raiding party from Newport, again led by

Leonard, "took a Rebel guard of sixteen men and some inhabitants with some stock. In this exploit he lost a Negro man (his property)." Hazard "then purchased part of an armed vessel and went on her himself, and was constantly employed in getting supplies and intelligence for the British army until Rhode Island was evacuated."[230] Hazard departed Newport with the British troops in October 1779, leaving behind his second wife, Eunice, and "seven young children, one them at the breast" in a "helpless condition."[231] Clearly, Hazard was fiercely committed to the Crown and fearless.

At about this time, the state of Rhode Island took action against Hazard and other Tories who had left the state and were aiding the enemy. At its session held in the first part of July 1780 in Newport, the General Assembly passed a law ordering that if Hazard or the other named men were found in the state, they should be apprehended, jailed and transported out of the state, and if any person so transported should be subsequently found in the state, they should "suffer the pains of death, without benefit of clergy."[232]

Hazard, still writing in the third person, recalled that "in July 1780, upon the French fleet's arrival at Rhode Island, he was employed by Captain Savage to go there to reconnoiter their station which he did." Hazard decided that he also "found it necessary to go on to the main for further intelligence," and took a small boat across Narragansett Bay, probably at night and to the South Kingstown coast. Before leaving, Hazard apparently had made arrangements for the British navy to send a small "boat to come for him in two days. But the weather coming up foggy, he was left there four days in the utmost danger of his life. The rebels having got intelligence of his landing, sent a party to take him, but by mistake they took another man and carried him to headquarters" at Providence. In the meantime, with the assistance of four local Loyalists, Hazard "procured a boat…in which he made his escape and got to the British fleet, when he made his report to Admiral Arbuthnot and General Clinton."[233]

Hazard's report included a detailed map of the French ships in Newport Harbor and a description of Rochambeau's defenses. The undated and unsigned map found in Clinton's files, in Hazard's handwriting and probably done around July 28, shows seven French warships in a crescent line in between Coaster's Harbor Island and Brenton's Neck and nearby artillery emplacements. His written notes stated:

> *5500 troops embarked and some*
> *2000 about so many sick, or at most not above 4,000 fighting men.*
> *Tomini Hill and little Tomini Hill*

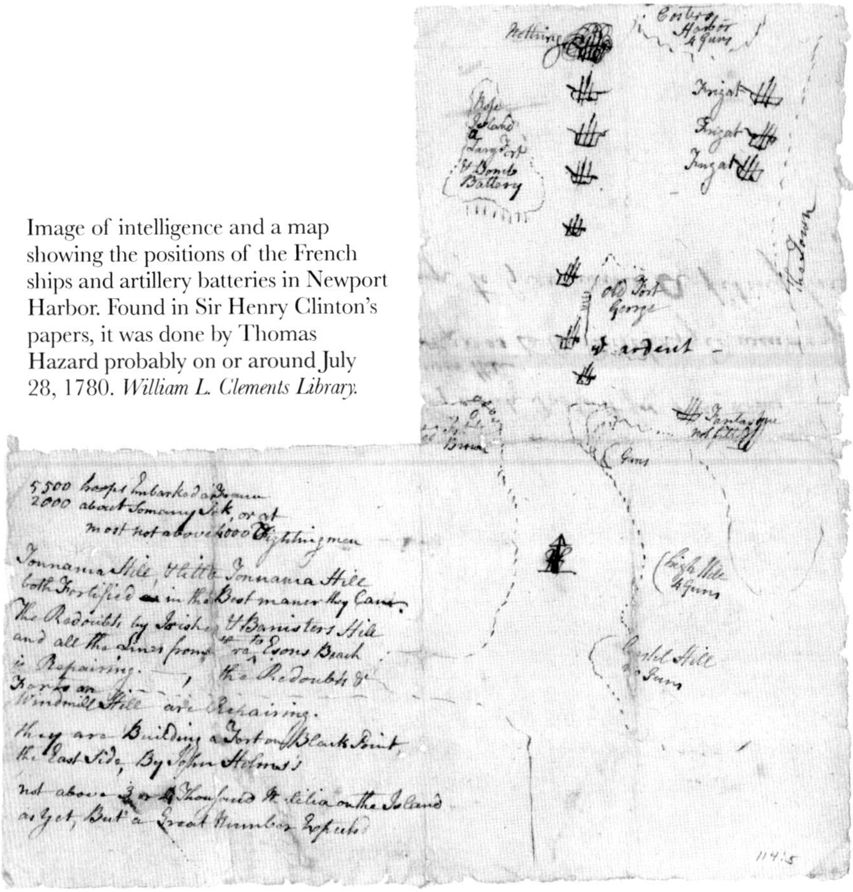


Image of intelligence and a map showing the positions of the French ships and artillery batteries in Newport Harbor. Found in Sir Henry Clinton's papers, it was done by Thomas Hazard probably on or around July 28, 1780. *William L. Clements Library.*

> *both fortified in the best manner they can.*
> *The redoubts by Irish's house and Bannister's Hill*
> *and all the lines from there to Eastons Beach*
> *are being repaired. The redoubts and forts on*
> *Windmill Hill are being repaired.*
> *They are building a fort on Black Point,*
> *on the east side, by John Holmes's.*
> *Not above 3 or 4000 militia on the island*
> *as yet, but a great many are expected.*[234]

On July 30, Captain Savage personally met with Clinton and conveyed Arbuthnot's opinion that the proposed attack "might be dangerous."[235] After receiving Captain Savage's report and holding a council of war, the British commander cancelled the attack. Clinton later wrote that he called off this operation against Newport because he had received a message from Admiral Arbuthnot of his "earnest desire [that] I should not proceed in the proposed attack because the enemy's troops were now strongly covered by works and a strong artillery."[236] After ordering his soldiers to disembark on Long Island, Clinton rushed back to New York City to confront the threat Washington posed against Kingsbridge.

On August 1, Hazard's written report arrived in New York City. Clinton interpreted Hazard's information in a letter to a colleague in England as follows:

> *The French, by an account just received, have completed all the works we had at Rhode Island and added new ones; are reinforced with 3,000 Provincials and as many Militia, all from New England Provinces; they have fortified the ground where I at first proposed landing in the Sakonnet Passage. In short, with 5 or 6,000 men, which is all I dare move from hence* [New York City], *I cannot undertake a siege opposed by 8 or 10,000 in ground where General Pigot with 5,000* [during the Rhode Island Campaign] *defended himself against 14,000 or more, and 12 sail of the line.*[237]

Meanwhile, in Newport, at 11:00 p.m. on July 30, General Heath received intelligence that "the British warships which were at Huntington have sailed westward" and that "part of the troops at West Chester had marched to New York." With the threat against Newport diminished, Rochambeau requested that Heath send many of the militia back home.[238] After Heath complied and issued the orders early on July 31, he received additional reports from General Washington and Connecticut's Governor Trumbull of Clinton's plan to attack Newport.[239] Even though this intelligence was merely repeating what Heath had already received from Webb, Hamilton, Babcock, Tallmadge and others, at Rochambeau's request, Heath reversed his position and called back the militia.[240] Despite leaving their farms during the all-important harvest season, militiamen flocked to Tiverton, causing Heath to exclaim to his commander in chief, "Perhaps a greater spirit never was discovered than has been on the present occasion."[241]

Arbuthnot's officers came up with their own idea for gaining more information about their adversaries in Newport. The British had captured several French naval officers during Clinton's recent victorious campaign at Charleston, South Carolina. Under the pretext of offering to exchange his captives, the admiral would send an officer to Newport under a white flag. Shortly after dawn on August 6, the HMS *Europe*'s first lieutenant, Josias Rogers, made his way in a barge toward Newport Harbor, with a white flag on its bow snapping in the breeze. Sailing into the harbor unopposed, Rogers saw at close range the enemy's seven ships of the line at anchor, with artillery batteries at Rose Island, Brenton Point and Goat Island. With no one halting him, Rogers had his small boat draw up alongside the massive *Duc de Burgoyne*, and he found it necessary to hail an officer on its deck. Finally, Rogers was brought before Admiral de Ternay, then gravely ill, and the two men politely worked out a prisoner exchange. Afterward, Rogers was even extended the courtesy of being allowed on shore, with a French officer in attendance, to visit friends in Newport.[242]

When Rogers returned to the *Europe*, he informed Arbuthnot that the French fleet was considerably smaller than had been supposed, that the crew of Ternay's flagship was in a poor state of discipline and that the French admiral himself was sick. William Green, Arbuthnot's aide, claimed afterward, with excessive optimism, "No doubt, if we had gone in, the whole enemy's fleet must have surrendered or been destroyed."[243]

Rogers also likely reported the increase in land-based artillery protecting Newport, including on several islands. Jean-François-Louis Crèvecoeur, then serving as a lieutenant in a French artillery company, recorded that the town's impressive coastal defenses included seventy artillery pieces consisting of "twelve 24-pounders, eight 16-pounders, eight 12-pounders, sixteen 4-pounders, two 8-inch howitzers, eight 6-inch howitzers, six 12-inch howitzers, six 12-inch mortars and four 8-inch mortars."[244]

Hazard's spying efforts were extraordinary, and Rogers's mission was a success, but they were for naught. By early August, Clinton essentially called off all plans to attack Newport. First, Admiral Arbuthnot, never a true supporter of Clinton's bold plans to invade Newport, lost interest when he saw for himself on July 26 the French warships anchored off Goat Island and the improved land defenses. He was further discouraged after receiving reports from Hazard and Rogers. "The enemy's fleet," the British admiral informed brigadier generals Edward Matthews and William Dalrymple in mid-August, "was too strongly posted—formed in a crescent and flanked by two islands [Rose and Goat], on which seventy large guns and mortars were mounted" and that "other batteries" could "rak[e] the ships also from different points," so that "his fleet would thereby be torn to pieces." The beleaguered admiral concluded, with exaggeration, "Nothing could be done after the first day of their arrival."[245]

Second, Clinton's fears that Washington would send a large force from New Jersey across the Hudson River to threaten British headquarters at New York City, in fact, materialized. As Clinton later observed, his foe, "by a rapid movement, had, with an army increased to 12,000 men, passed the [Hudson] River, and was moving towards Kingsbridge, when he must have learned that my armament [expeditionary force at Long Island] had not proceeded to Rhode Island. He (I apprehend in consequence of this) recrossed the river, and is now near Orange Town." On learning of Clinton's return to New York City on August 1, Washington pulled his army back from Kingsbridge and proudly informed the French that his diversionary thrust at Kingsbridge had forced the British to cancel their attack on Newport.[246] The French accepted Washington's assertion, which increased their respect for Washington's generalship.[247] In fact, according to the historian who has studied the matter most closely, the British decision to call off the attack was due mostly to their own miscommunications and missteps.[248]

Clinton's plan to trap the French expeditionary forces soon after their landing on Aquidneck Island came to nothing. In addition to Royal Navy ships losing track of Ternay's squadron on its way to Rhode Island and poor communications between Clinton and Arbuthnot, another important cause was the failure of Rhode Island Loyalists to provide timely information of the French arrival at Newport. On August 11, an anguished Clinton informed Arbuthnot that had intelligence been received "a few days after" the arrival of the French in Newport, "and had transports been ready for the troops, we might not have been too late."[249] Once he had another month to ponder the matter, Clinton conceded to Admiral Sir George Rodney, even if he was not being entirely honest about his beliefs back in July, "I naturally gave up all hopes" of a surprise attack on Newport, "when I found the enemy had at least fourteen days to prepare against it."[250]

Recent historians of the Culper spy ring have emphasized that the intelligence provided by the Culper spy ring led Washington to prepare a diversionary attack, which they say caused Clinton to drop his Newport plans and rush back to defend New York City.[251] As discussed above, this appears to be overstating the case. In addition, as this chapter has shown, word of Clinton's preparations came, as Hamilton wrote, from a number of "different channels."[252]

Earlier historians of the Culper spy ring credited it with alerting Rochambeau of Clinton's planned attack on Newport, allowing the French general time to thwart it.[253] As this chapter has shown, intelligence reports from Colonel Webb and Colonel Babcock arrived on July 24 and 25 at

Newport, ahead of the Culper spy ring's report sent by Hamilton. The intelligence brought by Webb, Babcock, the Culper spy ring and others did lead General Heath to call out the militia and likely spurred Rochambeau to hurry the preparations of Newport's fortifications. These improvements in Newport's defenses were noticed by the spy Thomas Hazard and British naval observers, which helped to discourage Admiral Arbuthnot from cooperating with Clinton, forcing the commanding British general to drop his plans against Newport. Accordingly, these American spy efforts played a substantial role in thwarting the British attack on Newport.

Clinton made a half-hearted attempt to renew plans for an attack in mid-August. Arbuthnot agreed to meet the army commander for a planning conference at the eastern end of Long Island, but when Clinton arrived there, after a grueling 120-mile coach trip, he was "exceedingly surprised" that Arbuthnot was nowhere to be found.[254] The admiral had received what he called "accounts (well authenticated)…that the enemy had, with circumstances of hurry and trepidation, completed their water and provisions and prepared to sail."[255] Ternay had done no such thing, but not wanting to lose touch with his rival, Arbuthnot ordered his entire squadron on August 17 to weigh anchor and sail toward Rhode Island. It is not known whether a Rhode Island secret agent had planted false intelligence of French plans, Arbuthnot had misused the information or a British spy had simply made a mistake.

Benedict Arnold, shortly after he had fled West Point for a British ship and exposed himself as a traitor, expressed to one new British colleague "his astonishment" at Clinton's "not having attacked the French upon their disembarking at Rhode Island."[256] Arnold's valuable intelligence had not been put to proper use. French officer Baron von Closen admitted: "If the enemy had been able to land during the first six days after the appearance of our fleet, we would not have been able to put up a very strong opposition, and our army would have risked a great deal. But with these endeavors, as with the fair sex, if the first moments of surprise are lost, all is over: *the favorable moments never return.*"[257]

After this debacle, Newport Tories would learn from their mistakes and improve the coordination of their espionage efforts. In short, they would be better at providing timely intelligence to Clinton and Arbuthnot.

## Mary Almy Hosts a Tory Spy Ring in Newport

Counterespionage efforts uncovered at least one clandestine operation in Newport. The following report was written, apparently by a French officer, on August 23, 1780.

> *Matters of fact, which will throw a light upon certain meetings in this Town, at night, in Thames Street. The third house at the left hand after the Parade* [south of the Brick Market]. *This house stands alone, is near the wharf, to which is an entrance by a garden door. There are in it many false secret entries. It belongs to Mr.* [Walter] *Chaloner. It is occupied by a widow who has three children, viz, a daughter, and one son who keeps a school in town, stays with her. Another son—tall fellow, lean complexion—stays at New York. This* [last] *man comes regularly, once a week and arrives in an open boat, and gets into the garden. At night a Negro woman lets him in the house by a back door. There he finds sometimes ten, sometimes fifteen persons who come half after night, and stay together till within an hour of day-break. They meet in a room up the stairs. During the meeting there are always sentries at the four corners of the house. At the window four or five days since a bit of* [colored] *cloth with red at a* [illegible] *window, that has a lookout on the port. It was taken up an hour before day break. As soon as it* [the cloth] *was taken in, three good looking men were seen going out of a door that looked like a case-door. They were dressed in blue. They passed through the garden and got into a boat which they found there. These meetings have been held regularly since the arrival of the French troops at Newport. They have been stopped two days since. It is thought they meet in another house, but we don't know where. The man who came from New York never stays in town above two days. In that space of time, he is never seen in town. He is only known to be there by the* [widow] *and other borders in the house.*[258]

The woman who was the focus of this note was Mary Almy, a staunch Tory who operated a fourteen-room boardinghouse on Thames Street, fronting the harbor.[259] Almy, the great-granddaughter of a former Rhode Island governor, was the wife of Benjamin Almy, who fought on the American side during the siege of Rhode Island. Mary stayed in Newport, with their children, during both the British and French occupations of Newport.[260]

During the siege of Newport in July and August of 1778, Almy kept a journal that revealed her strong character. Addressed as a letter to her husband, she warned him that her journal would "be done with spirit, for my dislike to the nation that you call your friends [Whigs] is the same as when you knew me."[261] After the arrival of Admiral d'Estaing and his French fleet off Newport Harbor, Mary wrote, "Cursed Frenchmen, they would not have come, had it not been for you" (meaning her husband and other Whigs).[262] With the failure of the French-American siege, husband Benjamin was unable to see Mary and their children.

From the account quoted above, it appears that Mary Almy hosted a den of Tory sympathizers, and possibly spies, in Newport. In her 1778 journal, Almy noted that her eldest male child, Benjamin, was then residing in New York City.[263] It was probably Benjamin whom the observer called the "son…a tall fellow" who "stays at New York" and "comes regularly, once a week and arrives in an open boat." When the above account was written, Benjamin was about to turn twenty-seven years old.[264] Was he a spy or courier for Clinton's intelligence network? He is reported to have died on September 12, 1781, in Newport.[265] The author does not know anything more about this potential spy ring or the cause of Benjamin's death.

After July 1780, as will be shown below, Newport Loyalists did coordinate their intelligence efforts. They tended to leave Newport one at a time with information about French plans and preparations and deliver it to the Royal Navy in Long Island Sound and the British army in New York City. This spy ring was probably led by Dr. John Halliburton, who also lived on Thames Street, perhaps at Almy's boarding house.[266] Halliburton's active role will be discussed later in this book.

## How Did Rhode Island Tories Convey Messages to Clinton?

How Thomas Hazard and other spies and couriers moved to and from Aquidneck Island is not definitely known. It appears that the following typically occurred. The courier would be dropped off by a British navy frigate onto Block Island, which the Royal Navy dominated throughout the war. From there, the courier would take a small boat about eight miles to the southern Rhode Island coast. He then likely would connect with local Loyalists in southern Rhode Island. If such Loyalists did not have a message to deliver, then the courier (or the local Loyalists) would travel by night on a small boat across Narragansett Bay to Aquidneck Island and meet with

Map showing the Rhode Island mainland, Block Island and Long Island. London, 1780. *Library of Congress.*

Loyalists in Newport. For the return journey, the courier would typically arrange on an assigned evening for the British ship captain to send him a boat at Point Judith, Watch Hill or some other spot on the coast of southern Rhode Island. If that failed, he likely would take a small sailing boat (either stolen or provided by friendly Loyalists) to Block Island and then to the eastern end of British-held Long Island. From there, he could ride a horse to New York City.

On August 3, 1780, Joseph Babcock of Westerly informed Rhode Island's governor, William Greene, "Last night, a man (since supposed a spy)" inquired "whether there was no way to cross over from the beach" at Westerly to Block Island. Babcock continued, "This fellow, though dressed like a tar [sailor] outwardly, yet was accidentally observed to be well-dressed underneath." Babcock added as a postscript, "Yesterday about 3 o'clock, a white bottomed boat was seen by Colonel [Joseph] Noyes and others hovering near the shore and other boats seemingly in concert with it. Afterwards the fog thickened so that we lost sight of them, but not doubted but that they were sent by the enemy for malicious purposes."[267]

Babcock intimated that the small boats had been sent from British frigates to pick up Tory couriers. In his journal entry for August 8, 1780, the French officer Baron von Closen wrote that the British frigates continued to sail outside Narragansett Bay in order "to leer at us and try to acquire some information from *Tories*, who slipped along the coast by boat and gave prearranged signals."[268]

The Tory activity on the southern Rhode Island shore eventually came to the attention of General William Heath, the American commander in the Rhode Island theater. In an August 30, 1780 letter to Governor Greene, Heath wrote, "I am informed by Captain Claghorn, who commands the guards of Point Judith and the several beacons between Tower Hill and Watch Hill, that there is a very frequent communication of boats between Block Island and the main [i.e., the Rhode Island mainland] at different places between Point Judith and Watch Hill under a pretense of coming to mill, etc." By that, Heath meant that those arriving from Block Island claimed that they were bringing wheat and corn to be milled at mills on the mainland. Heath continued: "British officers either of the army or navy in disguise, spies, or disaffected persons [i.e., Tories] may pass and repass with impunity and without the least danger of detection." Heath probably realized that Rhode Island lacked the resources to pay for constant patrols along the entire southern coastline. Still, Heath requested that at the least a law be passed requiring all operators of boats arriving from Block Island to check in at one or two posts so that those who were "suspected" of conveying information to the enemy could be "taken before proper authority."[269] Finally, on September 3, 1780, Heath took matters into his own hands, issuing an order forbidding "any boat or boats passing or repassing to or from the mainland to Block Island unless permission be first obtained."[270]

Heath's concern about the use of Block Island and the southern Rhode Island coast by spies is supported by a diary entry made by arch Tory William Smith when he was residing in New York City. On August 15, 1780, he recorded in his journal that two men had informed him that "last evening 4 men who had a few days ago left Newport came to Block Island and to Town [New York City], and report that no works were then raised by the French for want of the artillery, etc., at Boston."[271]

After Benedict Arnold's treachery was discovered in late September 1780, Washington ordered Heath to command at West Point on the Hudson River to replace the missing Arnold. No American general was assigned to replace Heath in the Rhode Island theater, making the fight against Tory spies in Newport less effective.

In December 1780, William Vernon, president of the Continental navy's supervisory board in Boston, and whose house Rochambeau was then using as his quarters, wrote his son in Newport about Newport's Tories. "I hope the military officers will take proper notice and care of them," Vernon wrote. "I think they should not be suffered to walk the streets; it seems necessary, to me, that they should be confined to their houses. I am persuaded that there are great numbers at Newport who will take every occasion of giving intelligence to the enemy, even at the risk of their necks. They cannot be too narrowly watched."[272]

Shortly after the arrival of the French in Newport, the port's town meeting requested the Rhode Island Council of War, "upon the approach of the enemy," to remove its known Tories to the interior of the state. The Council of War agreed.[273] The Newport town meeting voted whom to include on this "black list" of "disaffected persons" and to forward the list to General Heath and the Council of War. Whatever the reason, the Whigs would regret their failure to expel known Tories from Newport immediately after the arrival of the French.

## French Plans to Trap the Traitor Benedict Arnold Are Derailed by Spies

While Tory spies in Newport had let down Clinton and Arbuthnot by being tardy in informing them of the arrival of the French fleet in July 1780, their subsequent efforts were more successful. Indeed, a steady stream of Tories would depart Newport with critical intelligence that advanced the British war effort.

Benjamin Tayre had been the commander of Fort George on Goat Island in Newport Harbor, living in a "commodious house" with his large family, before being unceremoniously thrown out of his post and house by Whigs in 1775. When the British had evacuated Newport in October 1779, he had hid in barns and haystacks, until he was finally captured and confined in prison as a Tory. On January 19, 1781, he escaped custody, obtained a small sailing boat that he used to flee Newport and reached the Royal Navy fleet anchored at Gardiners Bay, at the east end of Long Island, more than fifty miles west of Newport. Tayre informed British military authorities that the new French fleet commander, Captain Chevalier Destouches (Ternay had died of illness), had ordered a store ship, some smaller transports and two warships to set sail from Boston to bring needed supplies to Newport.[274] Tayre added that Destouches had sent two ships from Newport to escort the convoy from Boston. Thrilled with this intelligence, Arbuthnot sent out three powerful warships to intercept the outgunned small French convoy. Then the French got lucky. A violent windstorm kicked up, but the French ships managed to avoid being wrecked or severely damaged.[275]

Colonel William Ledyard, the commander of the forts at New London and Groton, Connecticut, succinctly summarized what then happened to the warships dispatched by Arbuthnot in a January 27 letter to Rochambeau. Ledyard wrote that "since the Tories of Newport had informed Admiral Arbuthnot of the departure of our two ships…the latter had ordered two vessels of 74 [guns] and one of 64 to leave immediately from Gardiners Bay, where the fleet is anchored; but the violent gale from the south southwest… had beset them…and they had been obliged to put out to sea."[276] The British ships did not fare well in the storm: the seventy-four-gun HMS *Culloden* was driven ashore on Long Island and broke apart (its crew was saved), the ship of the line *Bedford* lost all three of its masts and the ship of the line *America* was blown off course. Spies sent from Rhode Island soon confirmed this loss.[277] The British were thus unable to benefit from Tayre's timely intelligence.

With French naval forces in Newport now roughly equal to their British counterparts off Long Island, an emboldened Destouches decided to send four warships on a mission to the Chesapeake Bay to capture Benedict Arnold, who, at the time, was commanding a British detachment holed up in Portsmouth, Virginia. Destouches decided not to embark any troops on the ships, which permitted a speedier departure. The four ships, under the overall command of Captain Le Gardeur de Tilly, slipped out of Newport on February 9. Because of the short preparation time, the Tory spies in Newport had no time to warn Admiral Arbuthnot. The mission, however, failed because the convoy was too small to make an impact and carried no French troops. Tilly did capture the forty-four-gun *Romulus* off the Virginia coast and bring it back to Newport, which improved the French navy's matchup of warships.[278]

Even before Tilly returned to Newport on February 24, plans were being made for another expedition to the Chesapeake Bay, this time involving the entire French squadron and 1,100 French troops. An elated Washington, who had pushed for this larger effort, made plans to visit Newport to hurry the expedition along.[279] Washington wrote orders to Lafayette, on his way to command troops outside of Portsmouth, to hang Arnold immediately when he captured him "due to his treason and desertion."[280]

Benedict Arnold, in uniform after promotion to major general of the Continental army. After a drawing by Swiss artist Pierre De Simitiere in Philadelphia. *National Archives.*

This time, Destouches and Rochambeau could not hide the bustling preparations taking place on Newport's wharves, and they became known to prominent Newport Loyalist William Brenton. Dr. John Halliburton, the Newport physician-Loyalist, sent Brenton on his way from Newport on

February 9. Four days later, Brenton reached Arbuthnot at Gardiners Bay in Long Island Sound with information that all of the French ships of the line were preparing to sail on an expedition with 1,300 troops on board and that their destination was supposed to be Chesapeake Bay. After being put ashore on Long Island, an exhausted Brenton arrived at New York City the night of February 16.[281]

Major Frederick Mackenzie, who had served on Aquidneck Island during its occupation by the British, but who now was assisting secret service operations in New York City, noted in his diary for February 17:

> *Mr. William Brenton, a native and inhabitant of Rhode Island, came in at 12 o'clock last night express from Gardiners Bay. He came off Rhode Island in a canoe 8 days ago with very material intelligence from a confidential person there (Dr. Halliburton) to the Admiral and General. 'Tis said the account he brings is that the French have detached a ship of the line and some frigates, with about 1,500 troops to the Chesapeake to attack Arnold, and intend going with a greater force immediately.*[282]

Brenton left his family behind in Newport and would not see them again until June 1783.[283]

Clinton recognized that if the powerful French naval force could combine with the American army outside Portsmouth, Arnold could be seized, along with his small army. On February 17, Clinton informed Admiral Arbuthnot, "As the enemy are supposed, from Mr. Brenton's seeming positive information, to have prepared 1,300 men for the intended enterprise, I have directed a very fair proportion of the troops to be in instant readiness to cooperate with any wishes or intentions of yours."[284]

In mid-February 1781, Dr. John Halliburton had a courier named Caleb Bruen take messages from Newport to General Clinton in New York City. Bruen hailed from Newark, New Jersey, and was formerly an officer in a New Jersey militia unit; now he served in Clinton's intelligence network.[285] Bruen's message was that three French brigades were seen boarding transport ships and that Washington was travelling to Newport to confer with Rochambeau.[286] This information reached British headquarters in New York City by February 19.[287]

Next, Thomas Hazard, the former North Kingstown resident who had engaged in spy operations from Newport in July 1780 and was now operating out of the east end of Long Island, went to work. Hazard sent Joseph Battey, who hailed from Exeter, Rhode Island, into Rhode Island via

Long Island and Connecticut. Battey had been taken into custody in May 1777 in Exeter and jailed for five weeks for corresponding with the British army. Eventually, he fled to Newport, where he remained, including after the British had abandoned the town in October 1779. After returning to Rhode Island, "at the risk of his life," as he later wrote, he obtained letters from Tories in Newport, including from Dr. John Halliburton, containing information that the French ships were about to sail to the Chesapeake. Battey then successfully left Newport on February 26 and brought this vital news to Admiral Arbuthnot at Gardiners Bay on the morning of March 2, adding that the French squadron was just waiting for a favorable easterly wind to depart.[288] Arbuthnot immediately forwarded this "undoubted intelligence from Rhode Island by a friend" to Clinton.[289]

Even the lethargic Admiral Arbuthnot wrote to General James Robertson in New York City on March 3 that "the blow meditating against General Arnold is of a deadly aspect" and that he was preparing for his fleet to follow that of the French.[290] On March 4, the British admiral ordered two of his ships to prepare to convoy troop transports carrying British reinforcements ready to assist General Arnold at Portsmouth.[291] Clinton's spy network continued to receive Thomas Hazard's intelligence reports from the eastern part of Long Island regarding the status of the French navy's preparations.[292]

Meanwhile, Washington, after travelling by horseback with a small entourage along the back roads of southern New England and spending the night at Little Rest (now Kingston), arrived in Newport on March 6 to meet with Rochambeau and to encourage Destouches's expedition. Baron von Closen, impressed with the American commander as were most of the French officers, proudly noted, "All the fleet was decked with flags and saluted him with 13 guns....Our army was in full dress....On the Long Wharf the troops lined the road to Mr. Rochambeau's house."[293] Destouches and his imposing French squadron, with General Washington watching, sailed out of Newport at sunset on March 8 and headed on a southward course for Portsmouth.[294] Destouches had waited for the wind to switch to the north late in the day, so that his ships sailing at night would have a better chance of evading British spy ships—a tactic that worked. The French and American plan was for General Antoine-Charles Viménil to land his 1,100 troops in Virginia to augment an American force stationed outside Portsmouth.

On March 9, Arbuthnot sent the frigates *Iris* and *Pearl* to reconnoiter the French ships in Newport Harbor. They returned the next morning with news of the French squadron's departure. Arbuthnot then immediately dispatched his fleet to the Chesapeake Bay.[295]

Contemporary drawing of French ships entering Narragansett Bay, circa the spring of 1781. *Historical Society of Pennsylvania.*

Arbuthnot thought that the entire French army was on board the French squadron headed for the Chesapeake, but Clinton determined otherwise on the basis of intelligence gained from two prisoners. The prisoners, who had been sailors on board the captured brig *Marquis de Lafayette* that had accompanied the French fleet, informed their British interrogators that the French transport vessels had remained in Newport Harbor.[296] Thus, Clinton accurately determined that Destouches could carry on his warships only about one thousand French troops.[297]

The key to the contest was whether the French could arrive at the Chesapeake Bay first, so that it could both establish a strong defensive perimeter in the bay and at the same time participate with American allies in an attack on Arnold at Portsmouth. Destouches decided to take a longer route into the ocean in order to avoid spy ships along the coast, while Arbuthnot had his ships take the more direct route hugging the coast. With their copper-hulled ships making them faster than their counterparts, the Royal Navy ships actually arrived at Chesapeake Bay ahead of Destouches. The two fleets fought a minor engagement on March 16, with the French getting the worst of it and being forced back to Newport.[298] The traitor Arnold remained secure in Portsmouth.

Newport's Tory spies had played a key role in this British victory. William Brenton's February 13 intelligence spurred Arbuthnot to gather his fleet for a speedy departure after the French, while Battey's timely March 2 messages led the British admiral to order his fleet to prepare to depart and to send his spy ships to Newport. Destouches made the mistake of waiting about a month to depart Newport after embarking his 1,100 troops on board his warships, giving Tory spies ample time to warn Arbuthnot and Clinton.

## While Newport Tories Develop Their Spy Network, the French Help the Allies Win the War

Thomas Hazard continued to supply British secret services with information from his Rhode Island spy network. On March 19, 1781, he reported that "by the best authority from Newport the French fleet had sailed two days before our fleet from Gardiners Bay."[299] On April 1, he passed along wildly inaccurate information gleaned from a "rebel" newspaper that Destouches's squadron, which had returned to Newport, suffered six hundred casualties in its minor action off the Virginia coast.[300]

Meanwhile, one of Clinton's most successful spies, Joseph Clark, penetrated as far as Warwick, Rhode Island, and in late March reported back to British headquarters in New York City about a rumor that French forces would soon be on a westward march to the Hudson River. On May 6, Lieutenant Carl Levin Marquard, on the staff of the British secret service, obtained information that troops were marching from Rhode Island toward the Hudson River.[301] Major Mackenzie wrote on June 2, "A Man came in this afternoon from Block Island, and said he was informed by a person who left Rhode Island [Aquidneck Island] on Thursday, the 31st of May, that the French troops had marched from Newport to the westward."[302] None of these reports was accurate—yet.

The British secret service, with the assistance of Rhode Island Tories, then developed an important spy in Newport, led by a man the British called "Our Friend in Rhode Island." Colonel Beverly Robinson and Captain George Beckwith, two key British secret service officers, sent their spy John Swan on March 10, 1781, "to procure intelligence" in Rhode Island. According to Swan's later report to Beckwith, Swan met with an old acquaintance east of New London, Connecticut, who warned him that "he would find much difficulty in travelling through the country," meaning that he could get picked up as a suspected Tory or spy. Swan's acquaintance brought Swan to another man, who, conveniently, had two brothers residing on Aquidneck Island. Swan and this other man then travelled to Scituate, a town in the northwest part of Rhode Island outside of Providence. This unknown Loyalist residing in Scituate had probably been banished as a dangerous Tory from his island or coastal home to this interior town.

Swan's new acquaintance then made his way surreptitiously to the coast of the mainland, where he took a boat, probably at night, over to Aquidneck Island, where he met with his two Tory brothers in Newport. He also "conversed with another gentleman of some consequence, who lives on that place"—probably Dr. John Halliburton. Swan's report was thorough and timely:

> *The French fleet is then almost fit for sea, the cannon embarking, as well as the ammunition and other stores. The French transports are at Newport and all the boats that could be assembled are collected there. The men-of-war have completed their watering, and a quantity of sheep and other livestock had been put on board. From every appearance, there is reason to suppose the French mean soon to quit Rhode Island; but it cannot be ascertained whether the troops are to accompany the fleet* [at sea] *or move into the country* [march by land].[303]

On about June 6, "Mr. Swan" brought a letter from "Our Friend in Rhode Island" that was dated May 31. The letter contained the stunning intelligence that "The F— [French] after consultation at Hartford with G— W— [George Washington] have come to a resolution of abandoning [Aquidneck] Island." The Newport spy noted that all of the army's baggage and impressive train of artillery were being embarked on board the French warships and transports. The Newport spy urged Admiral Arbuthnot to "bring his fleet to an anchor off the harbor's mouth," which would "keep the French army at Newport, which it is certainly in your interest to do."[304] General Clinton passed along this letter to Admiral Arbuthnot on June 6, with the recommendation that Arbuthnot "reoccupy your old station off Rhode Island," but the lethargic navy commander did not follow the advice of the spy or Clinton.[305]

As a result of the Hartford conference among the allies, it was agreed that Rochambeau should march the bulk of his army from Newport overland to New York City. Despite Washington's advice, Rochambeau decided to keep the remainder of the French forces—the French ships and sailors under their new commander Admiral Comte de Barras, just four hundred French regular troops under Brigadier General Marquis de Choisy, and the French artillery train embarked on transports—at Newport rather than remove them to the better-protected Boston Harbor.[306] On June 10, Rochambeau and his troops were conveyed by small boats to Providence.[307]

On the evening of June 13, another courier arrived at New York City, having departed Newport five days earlier. The courier conveyed intelligence that the French had embarked all of their cannon and some of their soldiers on board their ships in Newport Harbor, and that the remaining soldiers, some two thousand of them, were marching to West Point. The Loyalist

William Smith, who mentioned the arrival of this courier in New York City in his diary, also wrote that the courier had been sent by two Loyalists who were "members of the Rhode Island Assembly."[308] It is not possible to corroborate this shocking claim.

On June 19, "D.B." sent a letter from Newport to Captain George Beckwith. The author is confident that D.B. is the same person as "Our Friend in Rhode Island," based on D.B.'s reference to his intelligence provided on May 30 (really May 31) and on the same style of writing about detailed military matters. In this letter, the Newport spy provides intelligence that only 450 French soldiers and 1,000 militiamen remained in Newport to guard the seven ships of the line, the French transport vessels and the all-important French siege artillery. He added that no cannon were mounted in the port's forts. Characteristically, the Newport spy concluded, "The present situation of the French fleet left to the care of 450 men and 1,000 banditti [i.e., New England militia] points out at once what may be attempted."[309]

Who was "Our Friend in Rhode Island" or D.B.? He was Dr. John Halliburton, who was born in Scotland and sailed to Newport in about 1760 and stayed to develop a medical practice. In 1767, he married Susannah Brenton, the daughter of a wealthy Newport merchant, Jalheel Brenton, who would later become a captain in the Royal Navy during the Revolutionary War. With the outbreak of the rebellion, Halliburton was identified as an arch Tory.[310] In 1776, twenty-six Newport Tories were detained and ordered to sign an oath to support the Whig cause. Halliburton, along with another local physician, Dr. William Hunter, were among those detained and later banished from Newport. But they were later removed from the list and allowed to return—they were needed as physicians to care for the port's residents.[311]

During the British occupation, Halliburton served as a surgeon in British army and navy hospitals. He stayed behind after the British evacuated Newport in late 1779, in part because General Prescott had urged Loyalists to do so.[312] Thus, Halliburton, residing on Thames Street with a close view of Newport's wharves, would be in a prime position to provide British commanders with crucial intelligence when the French army and navy occupied Newport starting in July 1780.

Halliburton most likely authored the letters from "Our Friend in Rhode Island" and D.B. He was a well-read Scottish-educated physician who was one of the few men in Newport who could pen such well-written letters. Furthermore, in his application for a Loyalist claim, Halliburton stated that his spy activities ended in July 1781, which corresponds with the last

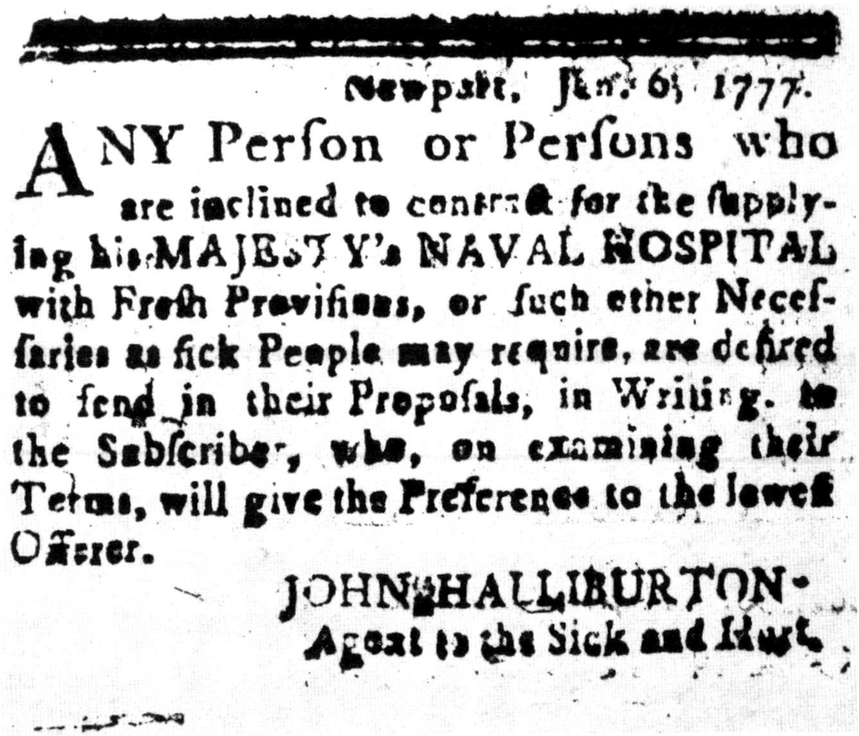


Advertisement by Dr. John Halliburton in the March 20, 1777 edition of the *Newport Gazette*. *Library of Congress.*

letter written by the Newport spy. Dr. Halliburton received compensation from General Clinton for his spy services and a letter of commendation from Captain George Beckwith, the head of Clinton's secret service after John André's hanging.

Halliburton was remarkably well informed of French plans, as were many Rhode Island civilians. The doctor gained additional information, as he later put it, by "becoming acquainted with" and gaining "the confidence of the principal French officers," including the Duc de Lauzun.[313]

Who was John Swan's contact east of New London, Connecticut, with two brothers on Aquidneck Island? According to Halliburton, he was thirty-nine-year-old John Robinson.[314] While there were a number of men named John Robinson in southern New England at this time, it appears that this John Robinson was the eldest son of William Robinson, a wealthy South Kingstown Quaker planter, owner of more than twenty slaves and former deputy governor of Rhode Island. He had four other sons: Thomas,

Sylvester, William and Christopher.[315] John resided in South Kingstown in 1774 but, with the start of the rebellion, apparently moved to near Stonington, Connecticut, which is not far from South Kingstown.[316] John's brother Thomas was a prominent Newport Quaker merchant. Thomas was also a staunch Tory, and for that reason, after the British evacuation of Newport, the Rhode Island Council of War ordered him temporarily confined to his home.[317] Another brother, William, was permitted by the Rhode Island Council of War to move to Newport in August 1777.[318] Thus, consistent with Swan's report, John Robinson had two brothers residing on Aquidneck Island. Thomas had an inside track for obtaining intelligence—during the French occupation of Newport, he quartered in his fine Washington Street residence Colonel Vicomte de Noailles of the Soissonais Regiment.[319] In addition, in 1779, Sylvester, as a result of his Tory sympathies, had been ordered to move from his South Kingstown home to the northeast interior town of either Gloucester or Cumberland, both of which are near Scituate, to which John Swan had travelled.[320] Thus, compelling evidence indicates that this John Robinson, son of William, was the one who assisted John Swan. However, this evidence is circumstantial and not conclusive.

Who was John Swan, who made dangerous trips to and from Rhode Island carrying Halliburton's correspondence? He might have been Elisha Beckwith of Lyme, Connecticut. In his application for a Loyalist claim, Elisha stated that he was retained by Colonel Beverly Robinson and Captain George Beckwith from May 8 to August 9 "to procure and send to them intelligence respecting the situation and strength of the French fleet lying in the harbor of Newport." Elisha passed on such intelligence to Colonel Robinson, until he was apprehended under suspicion of spying. He ultimately spent six months confined in the dreadful underground copper mine at Simsbury, Connecticut.[321]

In a July 8 letter to Captain Beckwith, Dr. Halliburton provided explosive intelligence that a French frigate had arrived from Boston on June 19 and had recruited ten pilots to guide Admiral Comte de Grasse's powerful French fleet to the North American coast. The Newport spy thought that de Grasse's object would be either New York or Virginia. Clinton immediately forwarded the following message to Admiral George Rodney and General John Vaughn: "On the 19th instant (June) a frigate arrived at Newport from Boston in the evening and, after taking ten pilots on board, sailed the next morning; and it is imagined they are bound to the West Indies to pilot a fleet from thence before the hurricane months."[322] Despite Halliburton's connections to French officers, he did not learn from them that when the new French naval commander, Admiral Comte de Barras, arrived at Newport, he carried news that de Grasse had sailed for the Caribbean (then known as the West Indies) with a large naval force that he would later take to North America to support joint American-French operations.[323] In addition, the commander of this frigate from Boston likely informed Barras of the ultimate destination of de Grasse—the Virginia coast—but Halliburton did not learn this crucial information either.

In the same July 8 letter, Dr. Halliburton repeated French and local newspaper reports that a French reinforcement was expected at Boston any day, but he accurately discounted them, in part because there were few preparations being made in Boston Harbor to receive a large fleet. He further advised that there remained guarding Newport only 450 French troops and 300 New England militia, with only eight artillery pieces in the battery at Goat Island "and not a gun or platform in any of the forts besides."[324]

Clinton agreed with his Scottish spy in Newport and made plans to assault Newport with a joint naval and army force, similar to the plans he made in July 1780. He believed, correctly in all probability, that "could the Rhode Island squadron be fortunately destroyed at the same time, I had no doubt but every hope and expectation of the enemy must be effectually frustrated."[325] If the French siege artillery had also been captured or destroyed, the siege of Yorktown might not have been successful. But Clinton delayed, waiting for the arrival of troop reinforcements from the Caribbean. And Admiral Graves, who had replaced the beleaguered Arbuthnot, was not overly keen on the idea.[326]

On August 17, 18 and 24, Clinton tried again with Graves, stating that he had "3,000 troops ready to embark at an instant, and every necessary arrangement prepared" for an expedition against Newport.[327] By August 23, Clinton had received intelligence of the French ships' imminent departure from Newport.[328] Clinton even met with Major Mackenzie on August 25 to discuss the attack, since Mackenzie had been stationed on Aquidneck Island for three years.[329] But by then, it was too late. As his troops finished embarkation the evening of August 28, Clinton learned from a spy arriving at New York City from the east end of Long Island, perhaps from Thomas Hazard, that Admiral de Barras and the French squadron, with the siege artillery on board and a favorable southeasterly wind, had left Rhode Island on August 25.[330] British commanders had delayed too long to benefit from Dr. Halliburton's valuable intelligence and advice.

After Rochambeau's troops left Providence and began their westward march on June 18, their progress was closely monitored by British spies in

Connecticut. It was widely believed that the French troops would join with Washington's Continental army for an assault on New York City. However, on August 14, Rochambeau received a letter from Admiral Comte de Grasse, who informed the general that he was sailing from the Caribbean for the Chesapeake Bay with his twenty-eight ships of the line and three thousand French troops. Rochambeau and Washington dropped their plans to attack New York City and surreptitiously marched south, fooling Clinton. They eventually turned up outside Yorktown, Virginia, as did a combined French fleet, one under Admiral de Grasse, and the smaller one from Newport under Comte de Barras. The joint French and American forces trapped the eight-thousand-man army under General Charles Cornwallis in Yorktown, forcing its surrender on October 20, 1781, which ultimately led to the American and French victory in the war. The Tory spies in Newport could not prevent this disaster for their cause, in part resulting from the August 25 departure of Barras's fleet from Newport for the Chesapeake Bay.

# *Epilogue*

## Dr. Halliburton's Harrowing Escape

While Yorktown effectively ended the war, its official end did not occur until the signing of the Treaty of Paris in France on September 3, 1783. Until that time, Tories still had to take great care.

In July 1781, Dr. John Halliburton's clandestine life began to unravel. According to Halliburton's post-war claim for reimbursement of his losses submitted to the Royal Commission in London, one of his secret messages was delivered by his Connecticut agent, John Robinson, to a man who passed himself off as a British intelligence officer. This man, named Dean, was, however, really an American spy. Fortunately for Halliburton, instead of immediately turning this information over to Major Tallmadge or General Washington, Dean saw an opportunity to make money by seeking a bribe from General Clinton for keeping Halliburton's identity a secret. But Dean was not able to reach British-held New York City to meet with the British commander in chief in time. When, in early September 1781, General Arnold commanded an expeditionary force that raided New London, Dean managed to meet with Arnold and demand money, but Arnold told him that "his intelligence would have made him a fortune if he had got it to New York in season, but it was then too late."

In June 1782, changing tactics, Dean arrived in Newport and began blackmailing Halliburton. Halliburton at first paid up, but Dean's demands became more frequent and pointed, and the physician further felt that "his secret" was "by no means safe in the hands of a man addicted to drink." Halliburton decided that he had to flee Newport, even though it meant leaving his wife and five children behind. After he sent messages to General Clinton, a British frigate was dispatched to pick him up off of Point Judith, at the southern tip of the southern Rhode Island mainland, but the plan failed. The backup plan, to send a boat to a prearranged place near New London, also did not succeed.

Halliburton may have visited John Robinson in or near Stonington. Probably from near there, on February 2, "in the depth of winter," with one man to assist him, he set off in a small boat to cross Long Island Sound to reach British-controlled Long Island. The travelers soon found themselves in a winter storm that tossed their boat so much that "they were in great danger of being lost," and the physician became violently seasick and suffered from stomach cramps. With the onset of bitterly cold weather, their boat then became "enclosed in a large body of ice." The poor doctor remained there for five hours, even though he was just one hundred yards from the Long Island shore, before finally getting to land. Several days later, the beleaguered Halliburton arrived in New York City and was taken to meet with General Clinton.

Clinton, understanding the valuable intelligence Halliburton had given him and realizing the harrowing journey the physician had just undergone, patiently listened to his spy rail against him for the "totally inadequate" offer of compensation that Halliburton had received for supplying his information. Halliburton tested the bounds of propriety when he personally told Clinton, "with a plainness natural to my character that if my intelligence which he had acknowledged to have received had been made proper use of, His Majesty's affairs would have worn a very different aspect." Despite the insult, Clinton gave the doctor 2,500 guineas and offered him a post in either the New York City or Halifax military hospital.[331]

Halliburton took the Halifax post. On April 8, 1782, the Rhode Island Council of War consented to a petition submitted by his wife, Susannah, for her to be transported to Halifax with her children.[332] The couple started a new life in Halifax, where the doctor barely managed to keep his family in a decent condition and died in 1807.[333]

# What Happened to Rhode Island's Master Spies?

As will be seen below, as with Dr. Halliburton, Rhode Island's master spies typically did not thrive after their spying careers ended.

## *Metcalf Bowler*

There is no indication that Clinton used Metcalf Bowler as a spy in 1780 or 1781, when the French occupied Newport. The commander in chief may have determined that he had better spies in Newport, and that the cost and hassle of dealing with Bowler were not worth the effort.

In 1780 and 1781, Bowler held a relatively minor post with the state Treasury Department. However, he was accorded the signal honors of serving on committees to draft a "congratulatory address" on behalf of the General Assembly of Rhode Island to both Rochambeau and Ternay and to deliver them to the French commanders.[334] One of his daughters,

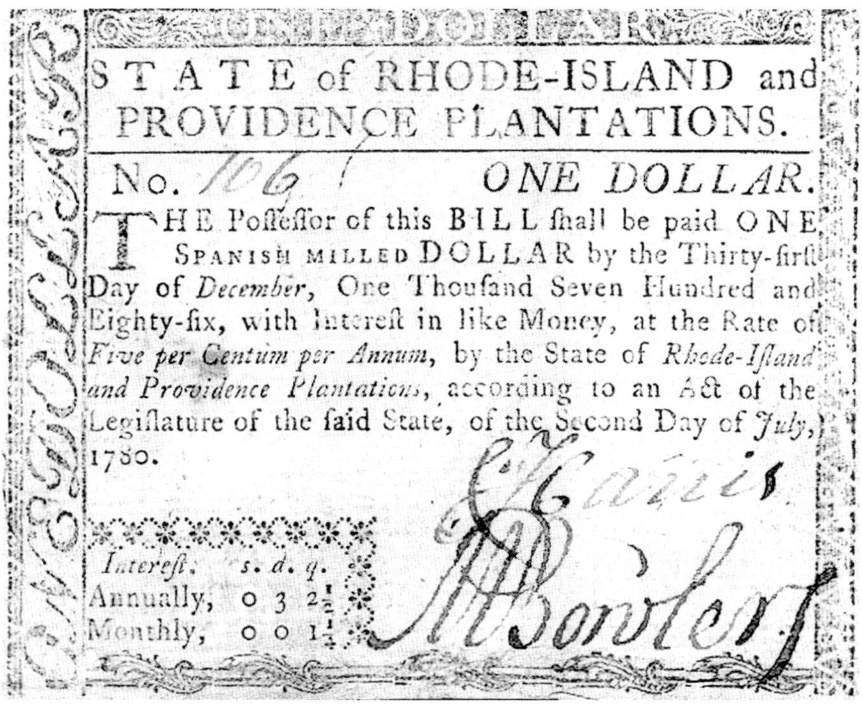


Rhode Island paper money, issued in 1780, signed by Metcalf Bowler. *Smithsonian Institute.*

Bathsheba, charmed French officers and ended up marrying one of them and moving to France.[335]

The secret turncoat not only never again held high office in Rhode Island; he also never again found financial success. His dry goods store in Providence did not thrive, and he had problems with creditors around 1784. He later opened a Providence boardinghouse. In 1786, he published *A Treatise on Agriculture and Practical Husbandry* and had the gall to send a copy of his eighty-eight-page volume to George Washington, who wrote a letter of thanks in return.[336] Washington likely would not have kept Bowler's book in his library at Mount Vernon, which was found there after his death, had he known of the Rhode Islander's treason. Bowler is also credited with having introduced the Rhode Island greening apple.

Bowler died in 1789. Fortunately for him, his role as a spy and traitor was not uncovered until the late 1920s, when researchers examining the papers of General Clinton found the incriminating correspondence between Bowler and Clinton.

## *Isaac Goodman*

After disclosing the existence of the secret Spencer's Expedition, Isaac Goodman was employed as a physician to a Hessian regiment and then to Wightman's Regiment of Rhode Island Loyalists. His wife "kept a public house for the officers" in Newport. Goodman joined in the British evacuation of Newport in October 1779, but a "rebel privateer" captured his boat. He was returned to Rhode Island, where he spent the next two years in misery in a Rhode Island jail. On his release, he made his way to England, where he lived a bleak life with his wife and two children, "destitute of the necessities for subsistence."[337]

## *William Taggart Sr. and William Taggart Jr.*

Rhode Island's general assembly, as a result of the Taggarts' losses sustained in spying for the American cause, found a temporary solution. In December 1777, it allowed the Taggarts to lease rent-free a Little Compton farm, known as the Sakonnet Point Farm, which had been confiscated from a Tory. Despite the coastal farm being vulnerable to attack by an amphibious raiding force, the desperate Taggarts rented the property.[338] The house also served as a guard post for sentries keeping an eye on the movements of British army and navy forces.

In May 1778, General Sullivan appointed William Taggart Sr. commander of a company of boatmen in charge of his department's flatboats and William Taggart Jr. as a captain of the same company. They continued in this service until William Jr. resigned in March and his father resigned in May 1779.[339] The Taggarts returned to their Little Compton farm.

In Newport, the Taggarts' spying activities were not forgotten. On the night of July 23, 1779, about forty Loyalist raiders from Newport took boats to Little Compton in an attempt to capture the Taggarts. During the surprise raid, one of the Taggart brothers tried to escape and was shot in the thigh. William Taggart Jr. painfully recalled years later that, as his brother lay on the ground writhing in pain, one of the Tory raiders caught up with him and "ran him through with a bayonet," killing him.[340]

The raiders brought their prisoners, Captain William Taggart Jr. and three privates who had been serving guard duty, aboard their schooner and carried them back to Newport. The prisoners were thrown in the former Newport County Jail. Taggart found himself in the same cell as Captain Benjamin Borden of Swansea, who had been captured in a Tory raid earlier that month.

The Little Compton, Rhode Island house where the Taggart family resided during the raid of July 1779. *Field, History of the State of Rhode Island.*

Taggart was at risk of being treated as a spy and hanged, since he had assisted his father's spying operations during Spencer's Expedition. On the night of August 10, Taggart and Borden successfully broke out of jail, were hidden for a time by one Nathan Brownell in Middletown, made their way to the sea shore where they made a makeshift sailboat from wood rails and sailed all night in the fog to safety on Prudence Island. From there, they were conveyed to Bristol.[341] Rhode Island general Ezekiel Cornell, who saw Taggart and Borden shortly after their arrival on the mainland, wrote General Gates that two men's feet were so swollen that neither one could put on a pair of shoes.[342]

William Taggart Jr., who became known as Judge Taggart, served as a member of the Middletown Town Council from 1786 to 1798 and as a deputy to the General Assembly in 1784 and 1798.[343] His family ran a ferry across the Sakonnet River at what is now Taggart Ferry Lane, but by the early 1830s, living with his wife and three daughters, he had fallen on difficult times. He was able to obtain a veteran's pension in 1832 and died on November 17, 1833.[344]

## *John Trevett*

Continuing aboard the Continental navy ship *Providence*, Captain Trevett, with twenty-eight marines, landed on the island of New Providence in the Caribbean and took possession of the island's two forts for a second time. After serving on various other ships, in June 1780, while a volunteer on the Continental frigate *Trumbull* during its fierce engagement with the British ship *Watt*, he lost an eye and was wounded in the foot. Following the war, at Newport, Trevett raised his family and worked as a carpenter "until infirmities, disease and blindness" forced him to stop. He died at Newport in 1823 at the age of seventy-six.[345]

## *Ann Bates*

The British spy Ann Bates continued to perform clandestine missions between 1778 and 1780. In September 1778, when she was on a mission infiltrating Washington's army, a deserter from the British Twenty-Seventh Regiment recognized her, but she was able to elude capture.[346] This event, however, led Ann to cease penetrating Washington's headquarters. Later, Ann was sent to escort from Philadelphia to New York City a female secret agent who had helped to turn Benedict Arnold. A series of safe houses provided shelter for the female spies until they came to the New Jersey shore of the Hudson River. When the boat sent to pick them up was delayed, the women had to stay hidden from Patriot scouts and were exposed to the elements for three days. Bates also provided her superiors with a report on Philadelphia shipping and the amount of flour to be found in its "rebel" mills.

Around April 1780, when her husband was sent to Charleston to participate in the successful siege of the city, Ann Bates traveled with the troops to South Carolina but did not engage in any further espionage activities. The couple sailed to England in 1781. Later deserted by her husband and in dire financial straits, she successfully petitioned the British government for a small pension on the basis of her wartime spying.[347]

## *Isaac Barker*

After the war, as Isaac Barker grew into maturity, the former spy became a public servant. He was elected in six different years as a deputy from Middletown to the general assembly from 1794 to 1815, and he also served as a member of the Middletown Town Council for nine terms between 1803 and 1816. Barker was said to have been the first in America to make a suit of clothes from silk that came from worms of his own raising.[348]

Barker submitted an application for a veteran's pension in 1833, but it was rejected, despite the important spying services he performed for the American war effort. It was rejected because he was a volunteer who had not enlisted in the Rhode Island or Continental forces, and volunteers were not, under the applicable statute, permitted to receive a pension.[349] After Isaac's first wife, Sarah, died in 1831, he married Wealthian Tripp the next year and then died in Middletown on September 7, 1834.[350]

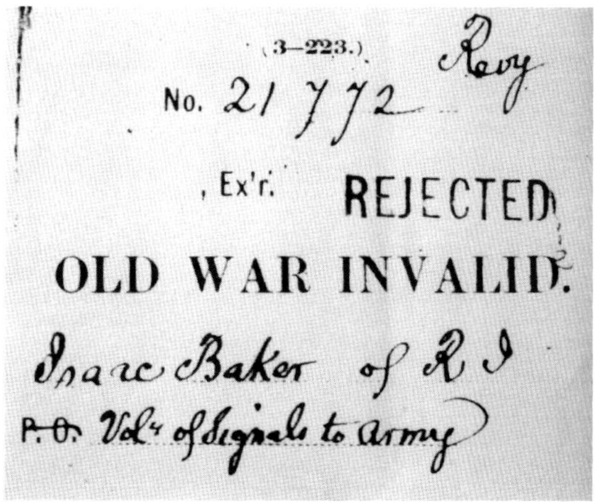
(3–223.)
Rev
No. 21 772
, Ex'r. REJECTED
OLD WAR INVALID.
Isaac Baker of R I
P.O. Vol^r of Signals to Army

Isaac Barker's application for a Revolutionary War pension, rejected. *National Archives.*

Sadly, the Great Rock, where Barker conducted

much of his spying activities, has been significantly reduced in size due to modern quarry operations.[351]

## *Thomas Hazard*

As Thomas Hazard was a known Tory who had fled Rhode Island in July 1780, he was banished from the state and much of his property was confiscated for sale. Hazard left behind a good-sized estate, including a 450-acre farm in North Kingstown, a fine house and lots in Newport, a sailboat and four slaves. According to Hazard's claim submitted to the Royal Commission in London, "To settle his affairs and in the month of July 1783," Hazard sailed on his own boat to Rhode Island, "but as soon as he arrived he was seized and imprisoned by order of the government and ordered to be transported" out of the state, "and his own vessel seized to discharge the expense of his transportation."[352] If Rhode Island authorities had discovered the extent of his clandestine espionage activities he had conducted during the French occupation of Newport, they might have treated him even worse than they did. Thomas's wife, Eunice, remained in Rhode Island for the duration of the war with their seven children, and was at least allowed to use some of the rents from her husband's land to support herself and her children.[353] After the war, probably around 1784, Hazard moved with his family to Prince Edward Island in Canada, where he died in 1804.[354]

# *Notes*

## Chapter 1

1. For Wallace's activities in Narragansett Bay, see Roelker and Collins, "Patrol of Narragansett Bay."
2. Robert Ferguson Loyalist Claim, British PRO, AO 13/68(1), 114, microfilm, Library of Congress.
3. The description of Chaloner's spy ring is from Walter Chaloner Loyalist Claim, British PRO, AO 13/21/94–97, ibid.
4. Diary entry, October 2, 1775, in Dexter, *Literary Diary of Ezra Stiles*, vol. 1, 618–19; see also sources discussed in Nagy, *Dr. Benjamin Church*, 96, n. 8 and Appendix D, 169–71.
5. Diary entry, October 2, 1775, in Dexter, *Literary Diary of Ezra Stiles*, vol. 1, 618–19.
6. Quoted in Nagy, *Dr. Benjamin Church*, 102–03.
7. Ibid., 104.
8. Ibid., 105.
9. Doctor Benjamin Church's Intercepted Letter, in Nagy, *Dr. Benjamin Church*, Appendix C, 166–68.
10. Ibid., 95, n. 7.

## CHAPTER 2

11. King George III to Earl of Sandwich, January 22, 1777, in Barnes and Owen, *Private Papers of John*, 172.
12. Memorandum Concerning the Country Around Rhode Island, Anonymous to H. Percy, n.d., Hugh Percy Papers, British Manuscript Project, reel Aln 26, Library of Congress.
13. H. Clinton to W. Howe, December 12, 1776, Henry Clinton Papers, v. 263, Misc. Correspondence, 1776–92, William L. Clements Library.
14. Memorandum Concerning the Country Around Rhode Island, George [no last name] to H. Percy, undated; Memorandum Concerning the Country Around Rhode Island, Anonymous to H. Percy, n.d.; Anonymous to H. Percy, January 22, 1777 (defenses in and around Providence); Anonymous to H. Percy, February 1, 1777 (Bristol), Hugh Percy Papers, British Manuscript Project, reel Aln 25, Library of Congress.
15. Military Intelligence Report, February 27, 1777, in ibid.
16. Jonathan Lawton Petition to the General Assembly Sitting at South Kingstown, n.d. (about March 1777), Society of the Cincinnati.
17. J. Spencer to N. Cooke, April 7, 1777, Letters to the Governor, Rhode Island State Archives.
18. Minute Book, Special Session, Superior Court, June 2 and July 16, 1777, file UB.1, F.14, Rhode Island Judicial Records Center. In his Loyalist claim submitted after the war, Ebenezer stated that he provided intelligence to the British in Newport, reporting to Lord Percy. Ebenezer Slocum Loyalist Rev. War Claim, British PRO, AO/45/12, microfilm, David Library of the American Revolution.
19. Diary entry, September 6, 1777, in Mackenzie, *Diary of Frederick Mackenzie*, 174.
20. Diary entry, November 8, 1778, in Greene, "Newport in the Hands of the British," 135.
21. Diary entry, August 15, 1779, in ibid., 173.
22. J. Lovell to G. Washington, March 24, 1778, with attachment dated February 28, 1778, in Twohig and Chase, *Revolutionary War Series*, vol. 14, 294–95.
23. Diary entry, January 1777, in Smith "John Trevett Diary," Appendix C, 327–28.
24. *New York Gazette*, April 14, 1777.
25. G. Washington to Congress, April 18, 1777, in Fitzpatrick *Writings of George Washington*, vol.7, 433–35 and n. 87.

26. W. Tryon to H. Percy, January 7 and March 17, 1777, Hugh Percy Papers, British Manuscript Project, reel Aln 26, Library of Congress.
27. *Providence Gazette and Country Journal*, May 24, 1777.
28. Diary entry, May 17, 1777, in Dexter, *Literary Diary of Ezra Stiles*, vol. 2, 160.
29. Bartlett, *Census of the Colony*, 187. State censuses conducted in 1777 and 1782 do not list a Jonathan Hart, which is some evidence that this was the man who was hanged. See Chamberlain, *Rhode Island 1777 Military Census* and Holbrook, *Rhode Island 1782 Census*.
30. Military Journal of Hugh Percy, February 10, February 12, February 27 and March 4, 1777, Hugh Percy Papers, British Manuscript Project, reel Aln 27, Library of Congress.
31. Baker, *Historical Sketch of North Kingstown*, 18 and 20; Cole, *History of Washington and Kent*, 120–21; Smith, *Civil and Military List*, vol. 1, 348.
32. Military Journal of Hugh Percy, April 11–12, 1777, Hugh Percy Papers, British Manuscript Project, reel Aln 27, Library of Congress.
33. G. Washington to J. Trumbull, April 12, 1777, in Twohig and Chase, *Revolutionary War Series*, vol. 9, 142–43. New London's *Connecticut Gazette* warned citizens to beware of fake Massachusetts bills as early as February 26, 1777.
34. *Newport Gazette*, May 29, 1777.
35. Diary entry, May 20, 1777, in Laughton, "Journal of Rear-Admiral Bartholomew James," 40. The author assumes that the "spies" that James mentions as having orders to pick up on the shore included Hart, as he later says that "the poor unhappy fellows that we went in quest of were taken and hung up immediately." James was mistaken in stating that two men were hung; only Hart was hanged. James's date is probably wrong; the dates in his journal are sometimes inaccurate.
36. Wanton Casey Recollection, in Cole, *History of Washington and Kent*, 127.
37. RI Council of War Records, May 16, 1777, Rhode Island State Archives.
38. Diary entry, May 17, 1777, in Dexter, *Literary Diary of Ezra Stiles*, vol. 2, 160.
39. *Connecticut Courant*, March 24, 1777.
40. Journal of Jethro Beebe, March 1777, Hugh Percy Papers, January–March 1777, British Manuscript Project, reel Aln 25, Library of Congress.
41. Scott, *Counterfeiting in Colonial America*, 258–59; *New Hampshire Gazette*, June 7, 1777 (May 29, 1777 execution).
42. *Providence Gazette and Country Journal*, May 17 and 24, 1777.
43. Diary entry, May 17, 1777, in Dexter, *Literary Diary of Ezra Stiles*, vol. 2, 160.
44. *Newport Gazette*, May 29, 1777.

## Chapter 3

45. Diary entry, September 4, 1777, in Greene, "Newport in the Hands of the British."
46. Diary entry, September 17, 1777, in Mackenzie, *Diary of Frederick Mackenzie*, 179.
47. Diary entry, September 29, 1777, in ibid., 186.
48. Diary entry, October 16, 1777, in ibid., 192.
49. Isaac Goodman Loyalist Claim, British PRO, AO 13/68(1), 289–99, microfilm, Library of Congress. For the dismissal of the charges against Goodman and his release from jail, see Minute Book, Special Session, Superior Court, June 2, 1777, file UB.1, F.14, Rhode Island Judicial Records Center.
50. Diary entry, October 17, 1777, in Mackenzie, *Diary of Frederick Mackenzie*, 192–94.
51. Ibid.
52. Ibid. For more on Spencer's Expedition, see McBurney, *Rhode Island Campaign*, chapter two.
53. Diary entry, October 30, 1777, in Mackenzie, *Diary of Frederick Mackenzie*, 206–08.
54. William Taggart Jr. Recollections, in "Autograph Memoir of William Taggart," *Literary Journal*, December 7, 1833; see also Cowell, *Spirit of '76*, 321–22.
55. Joseph Spencer Examination, n.d. (probably February 1778), in "Enquiry into the Cause of the Expedition Against Rhode Island," Robert Treat Paine Papers, reel 17, Massachusetts Historical Society.
56. Ibid; Cowell, *Spirit of '76*, 324; Bakeless, *Turncoats, Traitors and Heroes*, 280; Thompson, *Secret New England*, 203. The story is that the Hessian officers did not know that the maid, Gertrude Hegel, understood German. The author thinks this aspect of the story is unlikely. Thompson states that the Taggart's farmhouse "was on land that now is the Newport Memorial Park (national cemetery), off Vaucluse Avenue, .2 miles south of Green End Avenue." In the 1774 census, William Taggart Sr. is listed as having fourteen persons in his household, but no black persons. Accordingly, the author surmises that Cudjo was not Taggart's servant.
57. Diary entry, October 17, 1777, in Mackenzie, *Diary of Frederick Mackenzie*, vol. 1, 193.
58. Joseph Spencer Examination, undated (probably February 1778), in "Enquiry into the Cause of the Expedition Against Rhode Island,"

Robert Treat Paine Papers, reel 17, Massachusetts Historical Society; J. Palmer to J. Powell, October 21, 1777, in ibid.; Diary entry, October 20, 1777, Mackenzie, *Diary of Frederick Mackenzie*, vol. 1, 193; *Providence Gazette and Country Journal*, October 25, 1777; John Almy, RI, Revolutionary War Pension Application, National Archives Building (Almy was in the party of twenty-five men under the command of Captain Israel Church that scouted the area opposite Little Compton and captured two dragoons and brought them back as prisoners).

59. Major General Joseph Spencer Examination, n.d. (probably February 1778), in Enquiry into the Cause of the Expedition Against Rhode Island, Robert Treat Paine Papers, reel 17, Massachusetts Historical Society.
60. Diary entries, October 20 and 22, 1777, in Mackenzie, *Diary of Frederick Mackenzie*, 197–99; William Taggart Jr. Recollections, in "Autograph Memoir of William Taggart," *Literary Journal*, December 7, 1833.
61. See Depositions of Benjamin Morey, March 26, 1778; Ebenezer Raymond, March 26–28, 1778; Samuel Jones, March 27, 1778; John Wing, March 27, 1778; Joseph Jones, March 28, 1778; Seth Perry, March 30, 1778; Elijah Ellis, March 30, 1778; and others in Nathaniel Freeman Papers, Box 1, William L. Clements Library.
62. Deposition of Edward Davis of Boston, July 10, 1778, Box 2, ibid.
63. Thomas and Seth Perry Loyalist Claim, British PRO, AO 13/25/410-12, microfilm, Library of Congress.
64. Diary entry, March 25, 1778, in Mackenzie, *Diary of Frederick Mackenzie*, 259–60.

## Chapter 4

65. Henry Clinton Recollections, in Willcox, *American Rebellion*, 102.
66. F. von Lossberg to Unknown Major General, May 2, 1778, Redwood Library.
67. See R. Pigot to H. Clinton, May 27, 1778, in Davies, *Documents of the American Revolution*, vol. 15, 126–27; Special Report Attached to F. von Lossberg to Unknown Major General, May 31, 1778, Redwood Library.
68. Diary entry, May 22, 1778, Mackenzie, *Diary of Frederick Mackenzie*, vol. 1, 284.
69. Extract of a Letter from Newport, in *Rivington's Royal Gazette*, June 10, 1778.
70. Diary entry, May 24, 1778, in Greene, "Newport in the Hands of the British," *Historical Magazine* 4 (1860): 70.

71. R. Pigot to H. Clinton, May 27, 1778, in Davies, *Documents of the American Revolution*, vol. 15, 126–27; Diary entry, May 22, 1778, in Mackenzie, *Diary of Frederick Mackenzie*, 284; Extract of a Letter from Newport, in *Rivington's Royal Gazette*, June 10, 1778.
72. See McBurney, *Rhode Island Campaign*, 49–66.
73. Baker, *History of Warren*, 21.
74. Richard Holland Loyalist Claim, British PRO, AO 13/50/509, microfilm, David Library of the American Revolution.
75. *Bristol Phoenix*, May 25, 1878.
76. For the Rhode Island Campaign and the Battle of Rhode Island, see McBurney, *Rhode Island Campaign*, chapters 4 to 10.
77. Zebullon Weathers Deposition and Mansfield Allen Deposition, June 29, 1778, Revolutionary War Suspected Persons, #77, General Assembly Papers, Rhode Island State Archives.
78. General Orders, July 24, 1778, in Reed, "Orderly Book of Adjutant Silvanus Reed," 395.
79. General Orders, July 26, 1778, in ibid., 397.
80. J. Varnum to J. Sullivan, August 12, 1778, in Hammond, *Letters and Papers of Major-General John Sullivan*, vol. 2, 201–02.
81. General Orders, September 9, 1778, William Heath's Orderly Book, Revolutionary War Papers, RG M853, roll 3, no. 16, National Archives Building.
82. "A Spy's Report," undated, in Hammond, *Letters and Papers of Major-General John Sullivan*, vol. 2, 189–90.
83. M. Lafayette to C. d'Estaing, September 5, 1778, in Idzerda, *Lafayette in the Age*, vol. 2, 168–69.
84. M. Lafayette to C. d'Estaing, September 8, 1778, in ibid., 169.
85. J. Laurens to H. Laurens, September 24, 1778, in Laurens, *Army Correspondence*, 225–26.
86. Diary entry, December 7, 1778, in Mackenzie, *Diary of Frederick Mackenzie*, 430.
87. Undated note, probably by Major Duncan Drummond on June 27, 1778, Henry Clinton Papers 234:27, William L. Clements Library. This note has the same handwriting as in the British Intelligence Memorandum Book cited in the note below.
88. Undated entry (near end of book), British Intelligence Memorandum Book, MMC-2248, Manuscript Reading Room, Library of Congress.
89. The information on Ann Bates, unless otherwise stated, is from British Intelligence Memorandum Book, July 21–November 10, 1778, MMC-

2248, Library of Congress and British Treasury Papers, In-Letters, T1/611, British National Archives. Bakeless also relied on these sources. Misencik relied primarily on Bakeless. See Bakeless, *Turncoats, Traitors and Heroes*, 252–58 and Misencik, *Seven Covert Agents*, 78–86. To the author's knowledge, Bates's petition is not held by any library or archive in the United States. While the identity of the author of the intelligence book is not certain, it probably was penned by Major Drummond.

90. Journal, August 6, 1778, British Intelligence Memorandum Book, MMC-2248, Library of Congress.
91. Ibid., August 19, 1778.
92. Ann Bates's claim for compensation, March 17, 1785, British Treasury Papers, In-Letters, T1/611, British National Archives; quoted in Bakeless, *Turncoats, Traitors and Heroes*, 257.
93. Misencik, *Original American Spies*, 86.
94. McBurney, *Rhode Island Campaign*, 78.
95. Bakeless, *Turncoats, Traitors and Heroes*, 257; Misencik, *Original American Spies*, 85.
96. McBurney, *Rhode Island Campaign*, 76.
97. Undated entry (near end of book), British Intelligence Memorandum Book, MMC-2248, Library of Congress.

## Chapter 5

98. John Howland Recollections, in Updike, *History of the Episcopal Church*, 431.
99. Ibid.; Smith, *Civil and Military List*, vol. 1, passim.
100. Lovejoy, *Rhode Island Politics*, 54, 114–15, 118 and 120–21.
101. M. Bowler to Massachusetts Congress, April 25, 1775, in Force, *American Archives*, 389.
102. Rusticus to H. Clinton, September 15, 1778, in Clark, "Metcalf Bowler," 104–05.
103. Diary entry, August 16, 1778, in Cutler and Perkins, *Life, Journals and Correspondence*, vol. 1, 68–69.
104. M. Bowler to H. Clinton, December 12, 1776, in Clark, "Metcalf Bowler," 102–03.
105. Rusticus to H. Clinton, September 15, 1778, in ibid., 101, 103, 105.
106. M. Bowler to H. Clinton, December 12, 1776, in ibid., 102–03.
107. Rusticus to H. Clinton, September 15, 1778, in ibid, 105.

108. Ibid., 105.
109. Ibid.
110. Bartlett, *Records of the Colony*, vol. 8, 507.
111. S.H. to H. Clinton, n.d., in Clark, "Metcalf Bowler," 107.
112. H. Gates to R. Prescott, April 9, 1779, Horatio Gates Papers, New York Historical Society Library.
113. S.H. to H. Clinton, April 25, 1779, in Clark, "Metcalf Bowler," 101, 108.
114. For example, Gates appointed Bowler to sit on a three-man committee to examine the books of the commissary general to determine the state of the military stores. General Order, July 31, 1779, Lt. Col. William Smith Orderly Book, RG 93, M853, reel 5, roll 5, no. 32, National Archives Building. Gates also appointed Bowler the chair of a committee to make a list of the supplies left behind by the British in Newport and Conanicut Island. General Orders, October 29, 1779, Captain William Allen's Orderly Book, in Lovell, *Israel Angell*, Appendix II, 283.
115. S.H. to H. Clinton, October 2, 1779, in Clark, "Metcalf Bowler," 101, 115–16.
116. Ibid., 115.
117. S.H. to H. Clinton, April 25, 1779 and June 5, 1779, in ibid., 109–16.
118. Bakeless, *Turncoats, Traitors and Heroes*, 276 (not "of much importance"); Mahoney and Mahoney, *Gallantry in Action*, 80 ("not a good agent").
119. S.H. to H. Clinton, July 13, 1779, in Clark, "Metcalf Bowler," *Rhode Island Historical Society Collections* 22 (1930): 111.
120. S.H. to H. Clinton, September 15, 1779, in ibid.
121. G. Washington to H. Gates, June 27, 1779, in Fitzpatrick, *Writings of George Washington*, vol. 15, 324–25; G. Washington to H. Gates, June 30, 1779, in id., 343.
122. S.H. to H. Clinton, June 5, 1779, July 13, September 15 and October 2, 1779 in Clark, "Metcalf Bowler," 101, 108–11.
123. Rusticus to H. Clinton, October 22, 1778, in ibid., 106.
124. Clark, "Metcalf Bowler," 101. Jane Clark determined, by comparing handwriting and an examination of letters in Clinton's papers, that letters signed by "Rusticus" and "S.H." were in fact from Metcalf Bowler.
125. For Isaac Barker's spying activities, see Isaac Barker, RI, Revolutionary War Pension Application, National Archives Building, including not only his own application, but statements submitted by William Wilkinson and Hezekiah Barker; Seth Chapin, RI, Revolutionary War Pension Application, National Archives Building; Hezekiah Barker, RI, Revolutionary War Pension Application, National Archives Building;

Cowell, *Spirit of '76*, 181–84 (includes a transcript of Isaac Barker's pension application submission and recollections of conversations with Isaac Barker); Yarnall and Nicholson, "'Great Landscape in Miniature,'" 97–124, 245 (contains transcripts of excerpts from Isaac Barker's and Hezekiah Barker's pension applications and an article submitted by Isaac Barker published in the September 19, 1838 edition of the *Rhode Island Republican*; and its main text has the most detailed and accurate discussion of the applicable topography). See also references to Chapin's handling a spy on Aquidneck Island and intelligence reports in Horatio Gates Papers, New York Historical Society Library (see next note).

126. The thirty-eight letters are from Seth Chapin to Ezekiel Cornell, and from Cornell to Gates, between April 13, 1779 and October 24, 1779, in the Horatio Gates Papers, New York Historical Society Library.

127. Massachusetts, *Massachusetts Soldiers and Sailors*, 319.

128. The brig, with thirteen crew and passengers on board, had sailed from Newport but, due to contrary winds, had sailed up the Sakonnet River. When Chapin and his crew boarded the ship, the brig's crew ran up the ship's netting to escape from being hurt. J. Sullivan to H. Laurens, December 20, 1778, in Hammond, *Letters and Papers of Major-General John Sullivan*, vol. 2, 463–64; *Providence Gazette and Country Journal*, December 19, 1778.

129. Hezekiah Barker, RI, Revolutionary War Pension Application, National Archives Building. Hezekiah Barker, in his pension application, stated that he was "well acquainted with William Taggart, John Bailey and Isaac Barker, who lived in Rhode Island and were with him in the service while the British were on Rhode Island." Id. Captain William Taggart Jr. served as an officer of the boats in Rhode Island from May 1778 to March 1779, and thereafter did not serve as an enlisted soldier. William Taggart, RI, Revolutionary War Pension Application, National Archives Building.

130. For a discussion of the probable location of Chapin's guardhouse, see Yarnall and Nicholson, "'Great Landscape in Miniature,'" 101, 245, n. 11.

131. Ibid., 102–03.

132. E. Cornell to H. Gates, April 28, 1779, Horatio Gates Papers, New York Historical Society Library.

133. Isaac Barker report, *Rhode Island Republican*, September 19, 1838.

134. Yarnall and Nicholson, "'Great Landscape in Miniature,'" 105, 245.

135. Isaac Barker report, in *Rhode Island Republican*, September 19, 1838.

136. Isaac Barker Recollections, in Cowell, *Spirit of '76*, 182.

137. E. Cornell to Capt. Willis, September 6, 1779, in Horatio Gates Papers, New York Historical Society Library.
138. H. Gates to S. Adams, October 5, 1779, in ibid.
139. E. Cornell to J. Sullivan, January 13, 1779, in Hammond, *Letters and Papers of Major-General John Sullivan*, vol. 2, 488–89.
140. J. Sullivan to J. Powell, March 17, 1779, in ibid., 537.
141. Isaac Barker report, in *Rhode Island Republican,* September 19, 1838.
142. T. Tilghman to J. Sullivan, October 22, 1778, in Hammond, *Letters and Papers of Major-General John Sullivan*, vol. 2, 399.
143. J. Stark to J. Sullivan, December 6, 1778, in ibid., 456; see also J. Stark to J. Sullivan, December 5, 1778, in id., 453–54.
144. Bartlett, *Census of the Colony*, 9.
145. A List…of Inhabitants…Put on Board the British Prison Ship at Rhode Island October 1777, undated, box 123, folder 21, Newport Historical Society.
146. Diary entries, November 25–28, 1778, in Greenman, *Diary of a Common Soldier*, 132.
147. Regimental Order, January 15, 1779, Ebenezer Adams Orderly Book, Special Collections, University of Rhode Island Library.
148. S.H. to H. Clinton, June 5, 1779 and July 13, 1779, in Clark, "Metcalf Bowler," 111–12.
149. Diary entry, November 8, 1778, in Mackenzie, *Diary of Frederick Mackenzie*, 417.
150. Edward Matthew to H. Clinton, March 19, 1780, Henry Clinton Papers, 54:10, William L. Clements Library.
151. J. Gambier to G. Germain, September 29, 1779, in Davies, *Documents of the American Revolution*, vol. 17, 225–27.
152. J. Sullivan to J. Powell, March 17, 1779, in Hammond, *Letters and Papers of Major-General John Sullivan*, 536.
153. J. Sullivan to R. Prescott, January 1, 1779, in Documents of the Continental Congress, M332, R178, i160, f239-40, National Archives Building.
154. For the escape, see J. Garzia to J. Sullivan, February 19, 1779, in Hammond, *Letters and Papers of Major-General John Sullivan*, vol. 2, 517–18; *Connecticut Gazette*, February 26, 1779.
155. J. Stark to H. Gates, October 25, 1779, quoted in Moore, *Life of General John Stark*, 435.
156. See John Halliburton and Thomas Cutter Loyalist Claims, in Egerton, *Royal Commission*, 16–17.
157. G. Washington to J. Sullivan, August 4, 1778, in Hammond, *Letters and Papers of Major-General John Sullivan*, vol.2, 178–79.

158. See, e.g., J. Spencer to G. Washington, April 30, 1777, in Twohig and Chase, *Papers of George Washington*, vol. 9, 312–13; J. Sullivan to G. Washington, November 15, 1778, in Hammond, *Letters and Papers of Major-General John Sullivan*, vol. 2, 434; H. Gates to G. Washington, May 25, 1779, Horatio Gates Papers, New York Historical Society Library.
159. J. Sullivan to G. Washington, September 10, 1778, in Hammond, *Letters and Papers of Major-General John Sullivan*, vol. 2, 328–29.
160. Diary entry, July 24, 1777, in Mackenzie, *Diary of Frederick Mackenzie*, 157.
161. Examination of Persons Lately Escaped from Newport, May 24, 1779, attached to H. Gates to G. Washington, May 25, 1779, Horatio Gates Papers, New York Historical Society Library.
162. E. Cornell to H. Gates, September 19, 1779, in ibid.
163. E. Cornell to H. Gates, October 14, 1779, in ibid.
164. J. Williams to J. Sullivan, July 22, 1778, in Hammond, *Letters and Papers of Major-General John Sullivan*, vol. 2, 101.
165. H. Barns to Anonymous in England, January 5, 1777, quoted in Morgan, *Naval Documents of the American Revolution*, 862.
166. J. Laurens to J. Sullivan, July 27, 1778, in Hammond, *Letters and Papers of Major-General John Sullivan*, vol. 2, 128–29.
167. Diary entry, June 30, 1777, in Mackenzie, *Diary of Frederick Mackenzie*, 145.
168. See McBurney, *Kidnapping the Enemy*, chapters 5–7 and Appendix.
169. See ibid., 124, 217–18 (quoting General Assembly), and the accompanying notes.
170. Diary entry, July 11, 1777, in Mackenzie, *Diary of Frederick Mackenzie*, 150–51.
171. Military Intelligence Report, February 8, 1777, Hugh Percy Papers, British Manuscript Project, reel Aln 25, Library of Congress.
172. W. Howe to H. Percy, February 17, 1777, in ibid.
173. B. Arnold to G. Washington, February 7, 1777, in Twohig and Chase, *Papers of George Washington*, 267–68.
174. Military Intelligence Report, February 8, 1777, in Hugh Percy Papers, British Manuscript Project, reel Aln 25, Library of Congress.
175. Intelligence Sent to H. Percy, February 8, 1777, in ibid.
176. W. Howe to H. Percy, February 17, 1777, in ibid.
177. Military Intelligence Report, February 15, 1777, in ibid.
178. H. Barry to H. Percy, July 22, 1777, ibid., reel Aln 27.
179. P. Parker to N. Cooke, October 13 and 16, 1777, in Crawford, *Naval Documents of the American Revolution*, 138 and 181; P. Parker to N. Cooke, November 15, 1777, in id., 499; Diary entry, October 15, 1777, in Mackenzie, *Diary of Frederick Mackenzie*, 191.

180. Examination of Two French Sailors, September 1779, Horatio Gates Papers, New York Historical Society Library.
181. Examination of a Lady on the Board the Sloop *George*, May 24, 1779 and H. Gates to G. Washington, May 25, 1779, in ibid.
182. Diary entry, August 2, 1778, in Mackenzie, *Diary of Frederick Mackenzie*, 325.
183. Diary entry, August 19, 1778, in ibid., 362.
184. These kidnapping attempts and attacks are set forth in Diary entries, August 19–28, 1778, in ibid., 362–78; see also McBurney, *Rhode Island Campaign*, 160–61.
185. McBurney, *Rhode Island Campaign*, 160–61 and n. 115.
186. Diary entry, August 28, 1778, in Mackenzie, *Diary of Frederick Mackenzie*, vol. 2, 378.
187. Ibid.

## Chapter 6

188. Quoted in Kenny, *Town and Gown in Wartime*, 28.
189. Ibid., 28–29; R.I. Council of War Records, June 25, 1780, Rhode Island State Archives.
190. Henry Clinton Recollections, in Willcox, *American Rebellion*, 195 and n. 12; W. Smith Diary, September 28, 1780, in Sabine, *Historical Memoirs*, 335 (Clinton stated that he had learned about the expected arrival of the French fleet at Newport from Arnold and that it was Arnold's wish that the British army seize the port before the French did).
191. B. Arnold to J. André or G. Beckwith, Henry Clinton Papers, 104:49, William L. Clements Library.
192. Henry Clinton Recollections, in Willcox, *American Rebellion*, 195, n. 12.
193. Nolan, *Lafayette in America Day by Day*, 105.
194. Randall, *Benedict Arnold*, 504.
195. Henry Clinton Recollections, in Willcox, *American Rebellion*, 195.
196. J. Robertson to J. André, June 29, 1780, Henry Clinton Papers, 107:22, William L. Clements Library.
197. Extract of letter from H. Clinton to M. Arbuthnot, July 15, 1780, quoted in Willcox, *American Rebellion*, Appendix, 443–44.
198. Henry Clinton Recollections, in ibid., 198.
199. Quoted in Rose, *Washington's Spies*, 289.
200. Ibid.
201. Ibid, 289–90.

202. Ibid., 291.
203. A. Hamilton to M. Lafayette, July 21, 1780, in Syrett, *Papers of Alexander Hamilton*, 362–63 (the editor noted that the letter was sent from Preakness, New Jersey). For Washington's headquarters being at Preakness, New Jersey, on July 21 and 22, 1780, see general orders issued from headquarters on those dates in Fitzpatrick, *Writings of George Washington*, vol. 19, 222–23. For Hamilton writing his letter to Lafayette at 4:00 p.m., see id., 223, n. 91.
204. G. Washington to C. Rochambeau, July 27, 1780, in Fitzpatrick, *Writings of George Washington*, vol. 19, 268; G. Washington to W. Heath, July 31, 1780, in id., 282.
205. Henry Clinton Recollections, in Willcox, *American Rebellion*, 199; see also diary Entry, July 25, 1780, in Sabine, *Historical Memoirs*, 311 ("I perceived by it that on the news last Tuesday [July 18] from Montauk [in eastern end of Long Island] of the arrival of the French Fleet, 10th and 11th instant.").
206. C. Rochambeau to W. Heath, July 25, 1780, William Heath Papers, reel 16a, Massachusetts Historical Society; Kenny, *Town and Gown in Wartime*, 29 (quoting Marquis de Chastellux); Diary entry, July 1780, in Rice and Brown, "Crèvecoeur Journal," 18 (troops disembarked July 14 and 15); Diary entries, July 10–15, 1780, in Rice and Brown, "Verger Journal," 120; Diary entries, July 30, 1780, in Acomb, *Revolutionary Journal*, 28 (Closen's regiment disembarked on July 13); Count William de Deux-Ponts Recollections, in Abbass, *Rhode Island in the Revolution*, part 1, 469 ("The grenadiers and chasseurs were the first to land....They were followed on the 14th and 15th by the well troops, and the 16th, 17th, 18th and 19th were given up to landing the sick."). "Ternay had reported that he put ashore some 1,300 invalid sailors when the fleet arrived at Newport and that he could barely muster crews for his frigates...The land troops were also suffering severely from illness." Idzerda, *Lafayette in the Age*, vol. 3, 108, n. 5 (citing Ternay to Lafayette, July 16, 1780).
207. Kennett, *French Forces*, 49.
208. Quoted in Stone, *Our French Allies*, 204.
209. Henry Clinton Recollections, in Willcox, *American Rebellion*, 201; see also H. Clinton to M. Arbuthnot, July 22, 1780, in ibid., Appendix, 445.
210. H. Clinton to W. Eden, n.d. (probably in August 1780), quoted in ibid., 202, n. 9. Clinton may have been incorrect about the identity of the *Iris*'s captain as Hawkes. Major Mackenzie stated that he was George Dawson. List of British Ships and Their Captains, March 1781, in Mackenzie, *Diary of Frederick Mackenzie*, vol. 2, 485.

211. Henry Clinton Recollections, in Willcox, *American Rebellion*, 202.
212. Ibid., 201; extract of letter from M. Arbuthnot to H. Clinton, July 23, 1780, in id., Appendix, 445.
213. Henry Clinton Recollections, in Willcox, *American Rebellion*, 202.
214. For the arrival of Lafayette on July 24, see Heath, *Heath's Memoirs*, 259. None of Lafayette's correspondence indicates that the French general received Hamilton's letter prior to about midnight July 25.
215. S. Webb to J. Barrell, July 16, 1780, in Ford, *Correspondence and Journals*, vol. 2, 274–75. Another messenger included James Dean, a native of Groton, Connecticut, who was employed as an agent of the Continental Congress. Ibid.; Rice and Brown, *American Campaigns of Rochambeau*, vol. 1, 122, n. 12. Webb, in his July 16 letter, named as other intended passengers J. Broone, J. Wright and Merrill.
216. W. Heath to Admiral Ternay, July 24, 1780, William Heath Papers, reel 16a, Massachusetts Historical Society, with enclosure on Intelligence, July 24, 1780. Alexander Rose, in his fine *Washington's Spies*, at least addressed the possibility that the Americans may have learned about Clinton's plans from a source other than the Culper spy ring. He writes in a footnote, "About a week after the Culpers' report, Hamilton received a note from the mysterious agent 'L.D.,' who sounded as if he lived somewhere outside the city in what today would be Queens. Nothing more is known of him. It is officially dated July 21 in the Washington Papers, but it was written over the course of four days as the author updated it, the last entry being written on the twenty-fifth. The first section was written in the evening of July 21….[L.D.'s] report is accurate, but late, too late to be of any use." Id., 328, n. 88 (citing Intelligence Report, L.D. to G. Washington, July 21–25, 1780, George Washington Papers, Library of Congress). It does not appear that L.D.'s report was ever sent to General Heath in Newport, probably because it was duplicative of intelligence received earlier at Washington's headquarters. The mistake that Rose and other authors of the Culper spy ring made is that they focused on the documents in Washington's files and did not also examine the files of General Heath. After all, it was General Heath who commanded American troops at Rhode Island and who was being warned of an attack.
217. W. Heath to W. Greene, July 25, 1780, Letters to the Governor, Rhode Island State Archives. The time of the letter is set as 4:00 p.m. The reference to ten thousand British soldiers is also an indication that Heath at this time was relying on intelligence from Stonington, and not from the Culper spy ring, which had reported the number of British troops (more accurately) at eight thousand.

218. W. Heath to General Godfrey, July 25, 1780, William Heath Papers, reel 16a, Massachusetts Historical Society (timed 5:00 p.m.).
219. H. Babcock to W. Heath, July 24, 1780 (writing from Westerly).
220. H. Babcock to W. Heath, July 25 (writing from Stonington; this message was carried by Colonel Babcock's son).
221. W. Heath to J. Bowdoin, July 25, 1780. In the next letter Heath wrote, to Governor Greene, he said, "I send you the letter that Mr. Lafayette has received from an adjutant who is an intimate friend of General Washington [meaning Major Benjamin Tallmadge]. He asserts the certainty of Clinton's getting on board with 8,000 men to come and join the fleet."
222. See B. Tallmadge to G. Washington, July 22, 1780, George Washington Papers, reel 68, Library of Congress (from Croton on the Hudson River, 6:00 p.m.).
223. G. Washington to C. Rochambeau, July 21, 1780, in Fitzpatrick, *Writings of George Washington*, vol. 19, 223 (in Hamilton's handwriting).
224. S. Parsons to M. Lafayette, July 24, 1780, in William Heath Papers, reel 16a, Massachusetts Historical Society.
225. W. Heath to W. Greene, July 28, 1780, Letters to the Governor, Rhode Island State Archives. There are other intelligence reports in Heath's and Washington's files as well. One report found in Heath's files, which is undated and unsigned, is detailed and appears to have been written about July 22. Undated and unidentified intelligence, item #97, William Heath Papers, reel 16a, Massachusetts Historical Society. Elias Dayton, writing from Elizabethtown (now Elizabeth), New Jersey, also wrote an accurate report of British intentions on July 21. He probably had difficulty getting it timely delivered to Washington at his headquarters near the Hudson River. E. Dayton to Unknown, July 21, 1780, George Washington Papers, reel 68, Library of Congress.
226. G. Washington to N. Shaw, July 31, 1778, in Fitzpatrick, *Writings of George Washington*, vol. 19, 281.
227. Diary entry, July 28, 1780, in Gruber, *John Peebles' American War*, 398. Most of the British army troops had arrived at Frog's Neck on July 23, embarked on the arriving transports on July 24 and 25 and made it through Hell's Gate on July 25 and 26. Diary entries, July 23–26, 1780, in ibid., 396–97.
228. Captain Savage's Report to H. Clinton, July 30, 1780, in Willcox, *American Rebellion*, Appendix, 447.

229. Robinson, *Hazard Family*, 45.
230. Thomas Hazard Loyalist Claim, British PRO, AO 13.68(1), 308–24, microfilm, David Library of the American Revolution.
231. Resolution, February 1782, in Bartlett, *Records of the Colony*, vol. 9, 530.
232. Resolution, July 1780, in ibid, 13–42.
233. Thomas Hazard Loyalist Claim, British PRO, AO 13.68(1), 308–24, microfilm, David Library of the American Revolution.
234. Intelligence Report and Map, undated [about July 28, 1780], Henry Clinton Papers 114:5, William L. Clements Library. The hand that wrote this report also wrote two letters signed by Thomas Hazard, and all the correspondence was written on the same blue paper. See T. Hazard to O. De Lancey, March 19 and April 1, 1781, in ibid, 150:19 and 151:23.
235. Captain Savage's Report to H. Clinton, July 30, 1780, in Willcox, *American Rebellion*, Appendix, 447.
236. Henry Clinton Recollections, in Willcox, *American Rebellion*, 202.
237. H. Clinton to B. Carpenter, August 1, 1780, Henry Clinton Papers 117:4, William L. Clements Library.
238. W. Heath to J. Bowdoin, July 30, 1780, "Heath Papers," *Massachussetts Historical Society Collections*, 7th series, 5 (1905): 92; see also diary entry, July 30, 1780, in Acomb, *Revolutionary Journal*, 35. It appears that the British invasion fleet did not sail westward until the morning of July 31. Diary entry, July 31, 1780, in Gruber, *John Peebles' American War*, 398.
239. Diary entry, July 30, 1780, in Heath, *Heath's Memoirs*, 260. The most useful intelligence was forwarded by Governor Trumbull and Brigadier General Gold Selleck Silliman of Connecticut. Colonel Levi Wells of the Connecticut militia sent a report to General Silliman of a whaleboat man who operated in Long Island Sound and who reported that on the night of July 27, the British fleet was at anchor in the sound, it consisted of 150 sailing vessels, with eight thousand troops on board, and "had designs for Rhode Island." See L. Wells to G. Selleck Silliman, July 28, 1780, William Heath Papers, reel 16a, Massachusetts Historical Society; see also J. Trumbull to W. Heath, July 27, 1780, enclosing a report from Fairfield by J. Selleck Silliman, dated July 26, 1780, containing intelligence from Colonel Wells; G. Washington to C. Rochambeau, July 27, 1780, in Fitzpatrick, *Writings of George Washington*, vol. 19, 268–69; and G. Washington to M. Lafayette, July 27, 1780, in id., 269–70.
240. W. Heath to J. Bowdoin, July 31, 1780, "Heath Papers," *Massachussetts Historical Society Collections*, 7th series, 5 (1905): 93 (stating that he had just received correspondence from Washington and Trumbull; letter is timed 1:00 p.m.).

241. W. Heath to G. Washington, August 5, 1780, in ibid., 101.
242. William Green Memorandum, in Tilley, *British Navy*, 194–95.
243. Quoted in ibid, 195.
244. Diary entry July 1780, in Rice and Brown, "Crèvecoeur Journal," *American Campaigns of Rochambeau*, vol. 1, 18.
245. William Dalrymple Minutes of a Meeting between M. Arbuthnot and W. Dalrymple and E. Mathew, undated [probably August 19, 1780], in Willcox, *American Rebellion*, Appendix, 452.
246. G. Washington to M. Lafayette, August 3, 1780, in Fitzpatrick, *Writings of George Washington*, vol. 19, 315.
247. Kennett, *French Forces*, 50–51.
248. See Willcox, "Rhode Island in British Strategy, 1780–1781," *The Journal of Modern History* 17 (December 1945): 4, 311.
249. H. Clinton to M. Arbuthnot, August 11, 1780, in Willcox, *American Rebellion*, Appendix, 449.
250. H. Clinton to G. Rodney, September 16, 1780, in ibid., 457.
251. See, e.g., Rose, *Washington's Spies*, 190–92; Kilmeade and Yeager, *George Washington's Secret Six*, 124–26; Daigler, *Spies, Patriots, and Traitors*, 193–94.
252. A. Hamilton to M. Lafayette, July 21, 1780, in Syrett, *Papers of Alexander Hamilton*, vol. 2, 362.
253. See, e.g., Bakeless, *Turncoats, Traitors and Heroes*, 235–36.
254. Quoted in Tilley, *British Navy*, 196.
255. Ibid.
256. G. Damier to G. Germain, October 13, 1780, quoted in Randall, *Benedict Arnold*, 581.
257. Diary entry, July 30, 1778, in Acomb, *Revolutionary Journal*, 35.
258. Intelligence of a Joint Meeting of Disaffected Persons, from the Grand Provost Officer, August 23, 1780, William Heath Papers, reel 16a, Massachusetts Historical Society.
259. "Occupants of the Houses in Newport," *Newport Historical Magazine* 2 (1881–82): 41.
260. For a reference to Mary Almy keeping a boardinghouse in Newport, see introduction to her journal, "Mrs. Almy's Journal," *Newport Historical Magazine* 1 (July 1880): 17, and other references in her journal, such as for August 10, id., 27. There is an unsubstantiated legend that George Washington was once Mary's guest at the boardinghouse. Almy, "William Almy and His Descendants in America," paragraph 18, Benjamin Almy, Almy Descendant No. 1232–4.

261. M. Almy to B. Almy, September 2, 1778, in Almy, "Mrs. Almy's Journal," *Newport Historical Magazine* 1 (July 1880): 18.
262. Diary entry, August 3, 1778, in ibid., 21.
263. Diary entry, August 8, 1778, in ibid., 26.
264. Almy, "William Almy and His Descendants in America," paragraph 18, Benjamin Almy, Almy Descendant No. 1232–4.
265. Ibid.
266. Halliburton also lived on Thames Street. List of Quarters Occupied in the Town of Newport…during the Winter Quarters of 1780–1781, in Simpson and Simpson, "How Rochambeau Quartered his Army," *Newport History* 72–73 (Fall 2003–Spring 2004): 249–50, 119.
267. J. Babcock to W. Greene, August 3, 1780, William Heath Papers, reel 16a, Massachusetts Historical Society.
268. Diary entry, August 8, 1778, in Acomb, *Revolutionary Journal*, 36.
269. W. Heath to W. Greene, August 30, 1780, in Bartlett, *Records of the Colony*, vol. 9, 306.
270. W. Heath Order, September 3, 1780, William Heath Papers, reel 16a, Massachusetts Historical Society.
271. Diary entry, August 15, 1778, in Sabine, *Historical Memoirs*, 324.
272. W. Vernon to S. Vernon, December 1780, quoted in Stone, *Our French Allies*, 232.
273. R.I. Council of War Records, August 3, 1780, Rhode Island State Archives.
274. Benjamin Tayre Loyalist Claim in Coldham, *American Migrations*, 139 and AO 13/24/444-47, Foreign Copying Project, Great Britain, Library of Congress.
275. Benjamin Tayre Recollections, February 15, 1781, in Mackenzie, *Diary of Frederick Mackenzie*, vol. 2, 471.
276. Diary entry, January 27, 1780, in Acomb, *Revolutionary Journal*, 55–56.
277. Kennett, *French Forces*, 95.
278. Ibid., 96–97.
279. Ibid., 98.
280. G. Washington Instructions to M. Lafayette, February 20, 1781, in Fitzpatrick, *Writings of George Washington*, vol. 21, 255.
281. Intelligence Report from William Brenton, February 12, 1781, Henry Clinton Papers, 146:4, William L. Clements Library; Henry Clinton Recollections, in Willcox, *American Rebellion*, 251.
282. Diary entry, February 17, 1781, in Mackenzie, *Diary of Frederick Mackenzie*, vol. 2, 472.

283. In June 1783, the Rhode Island General Assembly allowed Brenton one week to visit Rhode Island for the purpose of removing his family to Halifax, Canada. Bartlett, *Records of the Colony*, vol. 9, 712.
284. H. Clinton to M. Arbuthnot, February 17, 1781, in Willcox, *American Rebellion*, Appendix, 488.
285. Bakeless, *Turncoats, Traitors and Heroes*, 248.
286. Sayle, "Chronology of Deception," 3. The author did not locate this information in the William L. Clements Library, but assumes it is there, as Sayle was a reliable historian of espionage in the Revolutionary War.
287. Diary entry, February 20, 1781, in Mackenzie, *Diary of Frederick Mackenzie*, vol. 2, 475.
288. Joseph Battey Loyalist Claim in Coldham, *American Migrations*, 135 and Foreign Copying Project, Great Britain, AO 12/100/499 and AO 13/68(I)/73-76, Library of Congress; Report of George Beckwith, of information from Beverly Robinson obtained from Thomas Hazard, March 10, 1781, Henry Clinton Papers, 149:4, William L. Clements Library. Robinson did not identify Battey, but the author suspects that the "man Hazard had sent into Connecticut" was Battey, based on Battey's Loyalist claim.
289. M. Arbuthnot to H. Clinton, March 2, 1781, Henry Clinton Papers, 148:12, William L. Clements Library.
290. M. Arbuthnot to J. Robertson, March 3, 1781, quoted in Randall, *Benedict Arnold*, 584.
291. M. Arbuthnot Orders to Captain Hudson, March 4, 1781, in Willcox, *American Rebellion*, Appendix, 491. Captain Hudson did not contact General Clinton about this matter until March 9. Extract of letter from Captain Hudson to G. Clinton, March 9, 1781, in ibid., 493. Clinton gave orders to Major General William Philips on March 10. Clinton Orders, March 10, 1781, in ibid., 495.
292. On March 10, Hazard, from other sources, reported to Colonel Robinson that "the French fleet had not sailed" by March 4, but that it was ready to sail, with French troops embarked on board, by March 5. He added that the ships could not have sailed before March 8, "when the wind became fair for them." (Hazard probably obtained the wind information from his own observations from the east end of Long Island.) He added, correctly, "The reports were that the French were certainly going to the Chesapeake to save Virginia." Ibid. This information was likely not timely enough to have been relied upon by Arbuthnot. Report of George Beckwith, of information from Beverly Robinson obtained from Thomas Hazard, March 10, 1781, Henry Clinton Papers, 149:4, William L. Clements Library.

293. Diary entry, March 6, 1781, in Acomb, *Revolutionary Journal*, 63.
294. Diary entry, March 8, 1781, in ibid, 65; G. Washington to M. Lafayette, March 8, 1780, in Fitzpatrick, *Writings of George Washington*, vol. 21, 331.
295. M. Arbuthnot to H. Clinton, March 11, 1781 (2:00 a.m.), Henry Clinton Papers 149:22, William L. Clements Library; G. Washington to M. Lafayette, March 11, 1781, in Fitzpatrick, *Writings of George Washington*, vol. 21, 333.
296. Intelligence Report from Two Naval Prisoners, March 18, 1781, Henry Clinton Papers 150:11, William L. Clements Library.
297. H. Clinton to W. Phillips, March 15, 1781, in ibid., 149:28.
298. Kennett, *French Forces*, 991–100 ("Tilly had made it to the Chesapeake in only four days. Destouches had been at sea for eight days when his squadron swung west for a landfall at Cape Henry"). For an account by a British lieutenant of the action, see Mackenzie, *Diary of Frederick Mackenzie*, vol. 2, 504–05.
299. T. Hazard to O. de Lancey, March 19, 1781, Henry Clinton Papers 150:19, William L. Clements Library.
300. T. Hazard to O. de Lancey, April 1, 1780, in ibid., 151:23.
301. Sayle, "Chronology of Deception," 4–5. The author did not locate this information in the William L. Clements Library, but assumes it is there. Marquard's May 6 report is consistent with the one reported by Major Mackenzie the same day. Diary entry, May 6, 1781, in Mackenzie, *Diary of Frederick Mackenzie*, vol. 2, 518.
302. Diary entry, June 2, 1781, in Mackenzie, *Diary of Frederick Mackenzie*, vol. 2, 534.
303. George Beckwith Report of Intelligence from John Swan, April 20, 1781, Henry Clinton Papers 152:44, William L. Clements Library.
304. Intelligence from "Our Friend in Rhode Island," May 31, 1781, Henry Clinton Papers 157:38, William L. Clements Library.
305. H. Clinton to M. Arbuthnot, June 6, 1781, ibid., 157:38.
306. Kennett, *French Forces,* 106; Count William de Deux-Ponts Recollections, cited in Abbass, *Rhode Island in the Revolution*, vol. 1, 479 (four hundred troops left behind).
307. Stone, *Our French Allies*, 391.
308. Diary entry, June 15, 1781, in Sabine, *Historical Memoirs*, 421.
309. D.B. to G. Beckwith, June 19, 1781, Henry Clinton Papers 159:34, William L. Clements Library.
310. Browne, "Newport's Revolutionary Physicians," *Newport History* 54:181, 8 (Winter 1981); Diary entry, March 1, 1777, in Dexter, *Literary Diary of*

*Ezra Stiles*, vol. 2, 131 (Halliburton received four out of five stars, with each star indicating degrees of Toryism).

311. Diary entry, July 13, 1776, in ibid., 22. Stiles further wrote in his diary for August 15, 1776, "Dr. Hunter and Dr. Halliburton departed Newport this day by order of the General Assembly." Ibid., 41. See also John Halliburton Loyalist Claim, in Foreign Copying Project, Great Britain, AO 13/24/241-50, Library of Congress (Halliburton was one of ten Loyalists banished from Newport; the General Assembly, by three votes, approved a petition to allow him to return to Newport on account of his important services as a physician).

312. John Halliburton Loyalist Claim, in Coldham, *American Migrations*, 140 and Foreign Copying Project, Great Britain, AO 13/24/241-50, Library of Congress.

313. John Halliburton Loyalist Claim, in ibid., AO 13/24/241-50.

314. Ibid.

315. Robinson Family Genealogical and Historical Association, *Robinsons and Their Kin Folk*, 23–37.

316. In the 1774 Rhode Island census, John Robinson had the profile typical of the Robinson brothers: a large family with seven black slaves or servants. Bartlett, *Census of the Colony*, 90. He does not appear in the Rhode Island 1777 military census or 1782 state census. See Chamberlain, *Rhode Island 1777 Military Census* and Holbrook, *Rhode Island 1782 Census*. He was back in South Kingstown by 1791. See Bartlett, *Records of the Colony*, vol. 10, 416.

317. R.I. Council of War Records, November 2, 1779, Rhode Island State Archives; see also Diary entry, March 1, 1777, in Dexter, *Literary Diary of Ezra Stiles*, vol. 2, 133; (Thomas Robinson received five out of five stars, with each star indicating degrees of Toryism).

318. R.I. Council of War Records, August 8, 1777, Rhode Island State Archives. William was listed as residing in Newport in 1774. Bartlett, *Census of the Colony*, 90. Stiles indicated that he was not a Tory. Diary entry, March 1, 1777, in Dexter, *Literary Diary of Ezra Stiles*, vol. 2, 131.

319. List of Quarters Occupied in the Town of Newport…during the Winter Quarters of 1780–1781, in Simpson and Simpson, "How Rochambeau Quartered his Army," *Newport History* 72–73 (Fall 2003–Spring 2004): 118, 249–50.

320. Bartlett, *Records of the Colony*, vol. 8, 589.

321. Elisha Beckwith Loyalist Claim, Foreign Copying Project, Great Britain, AO 13/26/37-38, Library of Congress.

322. Henry Clinton Recollection, in Willcox, *American Rebellion*, Appendix, 534, n. 71.
323. Idzerda, *Lafayette in the Age*, vol. 4, 156, n. 1.
324. Intelligence, July 8, 1781, Henry Clinton Papers 163:11, William L. Clements Library.
325. Henry Clinton Recollection, in Willcox, *American Rebellion*, 320.
326. Ibid.; H. Clinton to T. Graves, July 6, 1781, in id., Appendix, 539; T. Graves to H. Clinton, July 9, 1781, in id., Appendix, 542.
327. Extracts of letters from H. Clinton to T. Graves, August 17, August 18 and August 24, 1781, in ibid., 559–61.
328. Diary entries, August 23 and 28, 1781, in Sabine, *Historical Memoirs*, 433 and 435.
329. Diary entry, August 25, 1781, in Mackenzie, *Diary of Frederick Mackenzie*, vol. 2, 597–98.
330. H. Clinton to G. Germain, September 4, 1781, in Davies, *Documents of the American Revolution*, vol. 20, 222; Diary entry, August 29, 1781, in Mackenzie, *Diary of Frederick Mackenzie*, vol. 2, 603. Clinton did not mention the spy in his letter, but Mackenzie did in his journal.

## Epilogue

331. The story of Halliburton's last adventure is from John Halliburton Loyalist Claim in Coldham, *American Migrations*, 140–41 and Foreign Copying Project, Great Britain, AO 13/24/241-50, Library of Congress.
332. R.I. Council of War Records, March 27 and April 8, 1782, Rhode Island State Archives.
333. Browne, "Newport's Revolutionary Physicians," *Newport History* 54 (Winter 1981): 9, 181.
334. Bartlett, *Records of the Colony*, vol. 9, 85, 91, 144, 152–60, 198, 267,271, 335, 363 and 495.
335. Stone, *Our French Allies*, 330. Dr. Solomon Drowne of Providence saw Bathsheba in Paris in 1785, "as attractive as when conquering hearts in Newport." Ibid.
336. G. Washington to M. Bowler, August 19, 1786, in Abbot, *Papers of George Washington*, vol. 4, 220–21.
337. See Isaac Goodman Loyalist Claim, Foreign Copying Project, AO 13/68(1), 289-99 and AO 12/101/130-31, microfilm, Library of Congress.

338. Bartlett, *Records of Rhode Island*, vol. 8, 323; Cowell, *Spirit of '76*, 324; William Taggart Jr. Recollection, "Autograph Memoir of William Taggart," in *Literary Journal*, December 7, 1833.
339. It appears that Major Taggart did not pay sufficient attention to the flatboats. In an inspection on April 23, 1779, General Ezekiel Cornell traveled to Dighton, Massachusetts, and found seventy-one flat boats and 111 oars in poor condition. E. Cornell to H. Gates, April 24, 1779, Horatio Gates Papers, New York Historical Society Library. Taggart was relieved of his command shortly after this discovery.
340. William Taggart Jr. Recollection, "Autograph Memoir of William Taggart," in *Literary Journal*, December 7, 1833 and Cowell, *Spirit of '76*, 324.
341. Ibid; E. Cornell to H. Gates, August 11 and 13, 1779, in Horatio Gates Papers, New York Historical Society Library.
342. E. Cornell to H. Gates, 13 August 1779, in Horatio Gates Papers, New York Historical Society Library.
343. Arnold, *Historical Sketch of Middletown*, Appendix, iii–iv and ix–x.
344. William Taggart, RI, Revolutionary War Pension Application, National Archives Building.
345. Smith, "John Trevett Diary," *Marines in the Revolution*, Appendix C, 325.
346. Journal, undated (about September 30, 1778), British Intelligence Memorandum Book, MMC-2248, Library of Congress. See also Petiton of Ann Bates, March 17, 1785, British Treasury Papers, In-Letters, T1/611, British National Archives ("An English deserter who knew me gave information who I was so that I was obliged to make a precipitate retreat for fear of being taken as a spy.")
347. Ibid.; also see Bakeless, *Turncoats, Traitors and Heroes*, 258–62; Misencik, *Seven Covert Agents*, 86–91.
348. See Arnold, *Historical Sketch of Middletown*, Appendix, iii–iv and ix–x; Tilley, "Barker Ancestry," *Rhode Island Historical Magazine* 1 (1880): 47.
349. Isaac Barker, RI, Revolutionary War Pension Application, National Archives Building.
350. *Representative Men*, 623.
351. Yarnall and Nicholson, "'Great Landscape in Miniature,'" *Newport History* 70 (Spring 2000): 245, 114–15.
352. Thomas Hazard Loyalist Claims, British PRO, AO 13.68(1), 308–24, microfilm, David Library of the American Revolution; *Newport Mercury*, July 28, 1781 (auctioning of Hazard's land in Newport).
353. Bartlett, *Records of the Colony*, vol. 9, 530.
354. Robinson, *Hazard Family*, 45–47.

# *Bibliography*

## Published Primary Sources—Diaries, Letters and Others


Abbot, W.W., ed. *Confederation Series: The Papers of George Washington*. Vol. 4. Charlottesville: University Press of Virginia, 1995.

Acomb, Evelyn M., ed. *The Revolutionary Journal of Baron Ludwig von Closen, 1780–1783*. Chapel Hill: University of North Carolina Press, 1958.

Almy, Mary Gould. "Mrs. Almy's Journal: Siege of Newport, R.I., August 1778." *Newport Historical Magazine* 1 (July 1882): 17–36.

Barnes, G. R. and J. H. Owen, eds. *The Private Papers of John, Earl of Sandwich, First Lord of the Admiralty, 1771–1782*. Vol. 1. London: Naval Records Society, 1932.

Bartlett, John R., ed. *Census of the Colony of Rhode Island and Providence Plantations, 1774*. Lambertville, NJ: Hunterdon, 1984. First published 1854.

———. *Records of the Colony of Rhode Island and Providence Plantations in New England.* 10 vols. Brooklyn, NY: AMS Press, 1968. First published 1856–65 by A.C. Greene and Brothers.

Chamberlain, Mildred M., ed. *The Rhode Island 1777 Military Census*. Baltimore, MD: Genealogical Publishing Company, 1983.

Coldham, Peter W. *American Migrations, 1765–1799: The Lives, Times and Families of Colonial Americans Who Remained Loyal to the British Crown Before, During and*

*After the Revolutionary War, as Related in Their Own Words and Through Their Correspondence*. Baltimore, MD: Genealogical Publishing Company, 2000.

Crawford, Michael J. *Naval Documents of the American Revolution*. Vol. 10. Washington, D.C.: Government Printing Office, 1996.

Cutler, William P. and Julia P. Perkins. *Life, Journals and Correspondence of Reverend Manasseh Cutler*. 2 vols. Cincinnati, OH: Robert Clarke and Company, 1888.

Davies, K.G., ed. *Documents of the American Revolution, 1770–1783*. Colonial Office Series 12. 21 vols. Dublin, UK: Irish University Press, 1972–81.

Dexter, Franklin B., ed. *Literary Diary of Ezra Stiles*. 2 vols. New York: Charles Slocum Company, 1901.

Egerton, Edward H., ed. *The Royal Commission on the Losses and Services of American Loyalists, 1783 to 1785*. Oxford, UK: Roxburghe Club, 1915.

Fitzpatrick, John C., ed. *The Writings of George Washington from the Original Manuscript Sources, 1745–1799*. Vols. 11–24. Washington, D.C.: Library of Congress, 1934–38.

Force, Peter, ed. *American Archives*. 4th series, vol. 2. Washington, D.C.: M. St. Clair Clarke and Peter Force, 1853.

Ford, Worthington C., ed. *Correspondence and Journals of Samuel B. Webb*. Vol. 2. New York: Wickersham Press, 1893.

Greene, Fleet S. "Newport in the Hands of the British: A Diary of the Revolution." *The Historical Magazine* 4 (January 1860): 1–4, 34–38, 69–72, 105–07, 134–37, 172–73.

Greenman, Jeremiah. *Diary of a Common Soldier in the American Revolution, 1775–1783*. Edited by Robert C. Bray and Paul E. Bushnell. DeKalb: Northern Illinois University Press, 1978.

Gruber, Ira D., ed. *John Peebles' American War: The Diary of a Scottish Grenadier, 1776–1782*. Mechanicsburg, PA: Stackpole Books, 1998.

Hammond, Otis G., ed. *Letters and Papers of Major-General John Sullivan, Continental Army*. Vol. 1. Concord: New Hampshire Historical Society, 1930.

Heath, William. *Heath's Memoirs of the American War*. Freeport, NY: Books for Libraries, 1970. First published 1798 by Thomas and E.T. Company.

———. Heath Papers. Massachusetts Historical Society Collections. 7th series, vol. 4 (1904): 1–285.

Historical Manuscripts Commission. *Report on American Manuscripts in the Royal Institution of Great Britain*. Vol. 1. London: Mackie and Company, Limited, 1904.

Holbrook, Jay M., ed. *Rhode Island 1782 Census*. Oxford, MA: Holdbrook Research Institute, 1979.

Idzerda, Stanley J., ed. *Lafayette in the Age of the American Revolution: Selected Letters and Papers, 1776–1790.* Vols. 2–4. Ithaca, NY: Cornell University Press, 1979–81.

Laughton, John K., ed. "Journal of Rear-Admiral Bartholomew James, 1752–1828." In *Publications of the Navy Records Society*. London, UK: Navy Records Society, 1896.

Laurens, John. *The Army Correspondence of Colonel John Laurens in the Years 1777–78.* New York: New York Times, 1969. First published 1867 by Bradford Club.

"List of Quarters Occupied in the Town of Newport…during the Winter Quarters of 1780–1781." In Alan Simpson and Mary M. Simpson "A New Look at How Rochambeau Quartered His Army in Newport (1780–1781)." *Newport History* 72–73 (Fall 2003–Spring 2004): 91–121, 249–50.

Mackenzie, Frederick. *Diary of Frederick Mackenzie Giving a Daily Narrative of His Military Service as an Officer of the Regiment of Royal Welch Fusiliers During the Years 1775–1781 in Massachusetts, Rhode Island and New York.* New York: New York Times, 1969. First published 1930 by Harvard University Press.

Morgan, William J. *Naval Documents of the American Revolution.* Vol. 7. Washington, D.C.: Government Printing Office, 1976.

Nolan, J. Bennett, ed. *Lafayette in America Day by Day*. Baltimore, MD: Johns Hopkins Press, 1934.

Reed, Silvanus. "Orderly Book of Adjutant Silvanus Reed." *New Hampshire Historical Society Collections* 9 (1889): 364–414.

Rice, Howard C., and Anne S.K. Brown, eds. "Crèvecoeur Journal" and "Verger Journal." In *American Campaigns of Rochambeau's Army, 1780, 1781, 1782, 1783*. Vol. 1. Princeton, NJ: Princeton University Press, 1972.

Sabine, William H.W., ed. *Historical Memoirs of William Smith.* New York: New York Times and Arno Press, 1969. First published 1956 by W.H.W. Sabine.

Smith, Charles R., ed. "John Trevett Diary." In *Marines in the Revolution: A History of the Continental Marines in the American Revolution, 1775–1783.* Washington, D.C.: U.S. Marine Corps, 1975.

Smith, Joseph J., ed. *Civil and Military List of Rhode Island.* 2 vols. Providence, RI: Preston and Rounds, 1900–1901.

Syrett, Harold C., ed. *The Papers of Alexander Hamilton.* Vol. 2. New York: Columbia University Press, 1961.

Twohig, Dorothy, and Philander D. Chase, eds. *Revolutionary War Series: The Papers of George Washington.* Vols. 9 and 14. Charlottesville: University of Virginia Press, 1999 and 2004.

Willcox, William B., ed. *The American Rebellion, Sir Henry Clinton's Narrative of His Campaigns, 1775–1782.* New Haven, CT: Yale University Press, 1954.

## Published Secondary Sources—Books

Abbass, D.K. *Rhode Island in the Revolution: Big Happenings in the Smallest Colony*. Part 1: *A Chronology of the War in Rhode Island*. Part 2: *The Ships Lost in Rhode Island*. Part 3: *The Land Sites*. Part 4: *Bibliography and Appendices* (includes "Spies in the American Revolution," 463–72). 4 vols. 2nd ed. Washington, D.C.: USDI National Park Service, American Battlefield Protection Program, 2006. (Copies at RI State Archives, U.S. Naval War College at Newport and other Rhode Island libraries.)

Arnold, Samuel Greene. *Historical Sketch of Middletown, R.I.: From its Organization, in 1783 to the Centennial Year, 1876*. Newport, RI: John P. Sanborn and Company, 1876.

Bakeless, John. *Turncoats, Traitors and Heroes*. New York: Da Capo Press, 1975.

Baker, David Sherman, Jr. *An Historical Sketch of North Kingstown*. Providence, RI: F.A. Johnson, 1876.

Baker, Virginia. *The History of Warren, R.I., in the War of the Revolution, 1776–1783*. N.p.: privately printed, 1901.

Cole, J.R. *History of Washington and Kent Counties, Rhode Island*. New York: Preston, 1889.

Cowell, Benjamin. *Spirit of '76 in Rhode Island. Or, Sketches of the Efforts of the Government and People in the War of the Revolution*. Boston, MA: A.J. Wright, 1850.

Daigler, Kenneth A. *Spies, Patriots, and Traitors: American Intelligence in the Revolutionary War*. Washington, D.C.: Georgetown University Press, 2014.

Kennett, Lee B. *The French Forces in America, 1780–1783*. Westport, CT: Greenwood, 1977.

Kenny, Robert W. *Town and Gown in Wartime: A Brief Account of the College of Rhode Island, Now Brown University, and the Providence Community During the American Revolution*. Providence, RI: Brown University, 1976.

Kilmeade, Brian and Don Yeager. *George Washington's Secret Six: The Spy Ring that Saved the American Revolution*. New York: Sentinel, 2013.

Little, P.F. *Fragmentary Sketches & Incidents, in Little Compton & Tiverton, During the Revolution, and the War of 1812*. Little Compton, RI: Privately printed, 1880.

Lovejoy, David S. *Rhode Island Politics and the American Revolution, 1760–1776*. Providence, RI: Brown University Press, 1958.

Lovell, Louise Lewis. *Israel Angell: Colonel of the 2nd Rhode Island Regiment*. New York: Knickerbocker Press (G.P. Putnam's Sons), 1921.

Mahoney, Harry T., and Marjorie L. Mahoney. *Gallantry in Action: A Biographic Dictionary of Espionage in the American Revolutionary War*. Lanham, MD: University Press of America, 1999.

Massachusetts. Office of the Secretary of State. *Massachusetts Soldiers and Sailors of the Revolutionary War. A Compilation from the Archives (1896)*. Vol. 3. Boston, MA: Boston, Wright and Potter.

McBurney, Christian M. *Kidnapping the Enemy: The Special Operations to Capture Major Generals Charles Lee & Richard Prescott*. Yardley, PA: Westholme, 2014.

———. *The Rhode Island Campaign: The First French and American Operation in the Revolutionary War*. Yardley, PA: Westholme, 2011.

Misencik, Paul R. *The Original American Spies: Seven Covert Agents of the Revolutionary War*. Jefferson, NC: McFarland, 2014.

Moore, Howard P. *A Life of General John Stark of New Hampshire*. New York: self-published, 1949.

Nagy, John. *Dr. Benjamin Church, Spy: A Case of Espionage on the Eve of the American Revolution*. Yardley, PA: Westholme, 2014.

Pennypacker, Morton. *General Washington's Spies on Long Island and in New York*. Brooklyn, NY: Long Island Historical Society, 1939.

Randall, Willard Sterne. *Benedict Arnold: Patriot and Traitor*. New York: Morrow, 1990.

*Representative Men and Old Families of Rhode Island....* Vol. 1. Chicago: J.H. Beers, 1908.

Robinson, Caroline. *The Hazard Family of Rhode Island, 1635–1894*. Boston, MA: Compiler, 1895.

Robinson Family Genealogical and Historical Association. *The Robinsons and Their Kin Folk*. 3rd Series. New York: Robinson Family Genealogical and Historical Association, 1906.

Rose, Alexander. *Washington's Spies: The Stories of America's First Spy Ring*. New York: Random House, 2006.

Scott, Kenneth. *Counterfeiting in Colonial America*. Philadelphia: University of Pennsylvania Press, 1957.

Stone, Edward M. *Our French Allies in the Great War of the American Revolution*. Providence, RI: Providence Press, 1884.

Thompson, Edmund R. *Secret New England: Spies of the American Revolution*. Kennebunk, ME: David Atlee Phillips New England Chapter, Association of Former Intelligence Officers, 1992.

Tilley, John A. *The British Navy and the American Revolution*. Columbia: University of South Carolina Press, 1987.

Updike, Wilkins. *History of the Episcopal Church in Narragansett, Rhode Island*. Boston, MA: Merrymount Press, 1907. First published 1847 by Henry M. Oderank.

## Published Secondary Sources—Articles

Browne, Howard S. "Newport's Revolutionary Physicians." *Newport History* 54 (Winter 1981): 181, 5–34.

Clark, Jane. "Metcalf Bowler as a British Spy." *Rhode Island Historical Society Collections* 22 (1930): 101–17.

Roelker, W.G., and Clarkson A. Collins III. "The Patrol of Narragansett Bay (1774–76), by HMS *Rose*, Captain James Wallace." *Rhode Island History* 7 (January 1948): 1, 12–15 and 90–95; 8 (April 1949): 2, 45–63; 8 (July 1949): 3, 77–83; and 9 (January 1950): 1, 11–23.

Tilley, Risbrough Iammett. "The Barker Ancestry." *Rhode Island Historical Magazine* 1 (July 1880): 37–50.

William B. Willcox. "Rhode Island in British Strategy, 1780–1781." *Journal of Modern History* 17 (1945): 304–31.

Yarnall, James L. and Natalie N. Nicholson. "'Great Landscape in Miniature': Great Rock, Paradise Farm, and the Barkers of Middletown." *Newport History* 70 (Spring 2000): 97–124, 245.

## Unpublished Records

Almy, Merwin F. "William Almy and His Descendants in America." *News.almy.us*. http://news.almy.us/book/index.html.

Sayle, Edward F. "Chronology of a Deception, George Washington's Deception Operations Prior to the Victory at Yorktown." Declassified U.S. government report, n.d. (accessed on August 2014 by searching in Google the terms "Edwin F. Sayle" and "Deception"; Mr. Sayle was an author of several works on the history of espionage activities.)

## Newspapers and Magazines

*Bristol Phoenix* (Bristol, RI), 1878.

*Connecticut Courant* (Hartford, CT), 1777.

*Connecticut Gazette* (New London, CT), 1777–79.

*The Literary Journal, and Weekly Register of Science and the Arts* (Providence, RI), 1833.

*Massachusetts Spy* (Worcester, MA), 1780.

*New Hampshire Gazette* (Portsmouth, NH), 1777.

*Newport Gazette* (Newport, RI), 1777–78. Originals at Rhode Island Historical Society and Library of Congress.
*Newport Mercury* (Newport, RI), 1767 and 1781.
*New York Gazette and Weekly Mercury* 1777.
*Providence Gazette and Country Journal* (Providence, RI), 1777–78.
*Rhode Island Republican* (Providence, RI), 1838.
Rivington's *Royal Gazette* (New York), 1778.

## Unpublished Sources—Original Sources

British National Archives (London, UK):
Treasury Papers. In-Letters. T1/611. March 17, 1785.
David Library of the American Revolution (Washington Crossing, PA):
British Loyalist Revolutionary War Claims. Microfilm.
Library of Congress, Manuscript Reading Room (Washington, D.C.):
British Intelligence Memorandum Book. MMC-2248.
George Washington Papers.
Foreign Copying Project, Great Britain.
Library of Congress, Microform Reading Room (Washington, D.C.):
Hugh Percy Papers. Duke of Northumberland Library at Alnwick Castle. British Manuscript Project. Letters and Papers relating to the American War. F286/49 to F289/52. Microfilm reels Aln 25, 26 and 27.
Massachusetts Historical Society (Boston, MA):
Robert Treat Paine Papers. "Enquiry into the Causes and Failures of the Expedition Against Rhode Island."
William Heath Papers. Microfilm.
National Archives Building (Washington, D.C.):
Documents of the Continental Congress.
Revolutionary War Pension Application Records.
Orderly Books.
Newport Historical Society (Newport, RI):
List…of Inhabitants…Put on Board the British Prison Ship at Rhode Island.
New York Historical Society Library (New York, NY):
Horatio Gates Papers.
Redwood Library and Athenaeum (Newport, RI):
General Friedrich Wilhelm von Lossberg Letters. 1776–79. Typed manuscript.

Rhode Island Judicial Records Center (Pawtucket, RI):
Minute Book. Special Session, Superior Court. June 2, 1777.
Rhode Island State Archives (Providence, RI):
Council of War Records. 1776-1781.
Letters from the Governor of Rhode Island. 1776–79.
Letters to the Governor of Rhode Island. 1776–79.
Military Papers, Revolutionary War. 1775–1782.
Society of the Cincinnati (Washington, D.C.):
Jonathan Lawton Petition.
University of Rhode Island Library, Special Collections (Kingston, RI):
Ebenezer Adams Orderly Book.
William L. Clements Library, University of Michigan (Ann Arbor, MI):
Henry Clinton Papers.
Nathaniel Freeman Papers.

# Index

## S



## T



## U



## V



## W



## Y

# *About the Author*

After growing up in Kingston, Rhode Island, and attending Brown University, Christian McBurney now resides in the Washington, D.C., area. He is an independent historian whose work emphasizes the Revolutionary War and Rhode Island. He has authored most recently *Kidnapping the Enemy: The Special Operations to Capture Generals Charles Lee and Richard Prescott* (Westholme, 2014), and he previously authored *The Rhode Island Campaign: The First French and American Operation in the Revolutionary War* (Westholme, 2011). For more information on these and his other books, see www.christianmcburney.com.